# *The Keys to My House*
## *A Gaza Diary*

Sami al-Ajrami, *with* Anna Lombardi

# THE KEYS TO MY HOUSE

## A GAZA DIARY

*Translated by* Jim Hicks, *with* Anna Botta

An imprint of Interlink Publishing Group, Inc.
Northampton, Massachusetts

First published in 2026 by

Olive Branch Press
An imprint of Interlink Publishing Group, Inc.
46 Crosby Street, Northampton, MA 01060
www.interlinkbooks.com



Published in Italy as *Le chiavi di casa: Un diario da Gaza* by Mondadori, Italy



Library of Congress Cataloging-in-Publication data available
ISBN-13: 978-1-62371-554-0

Printed and bound in the United States of America

# Contents

**JANUARY**



**FEBRUARY**



**MARCH**



**APRIL**

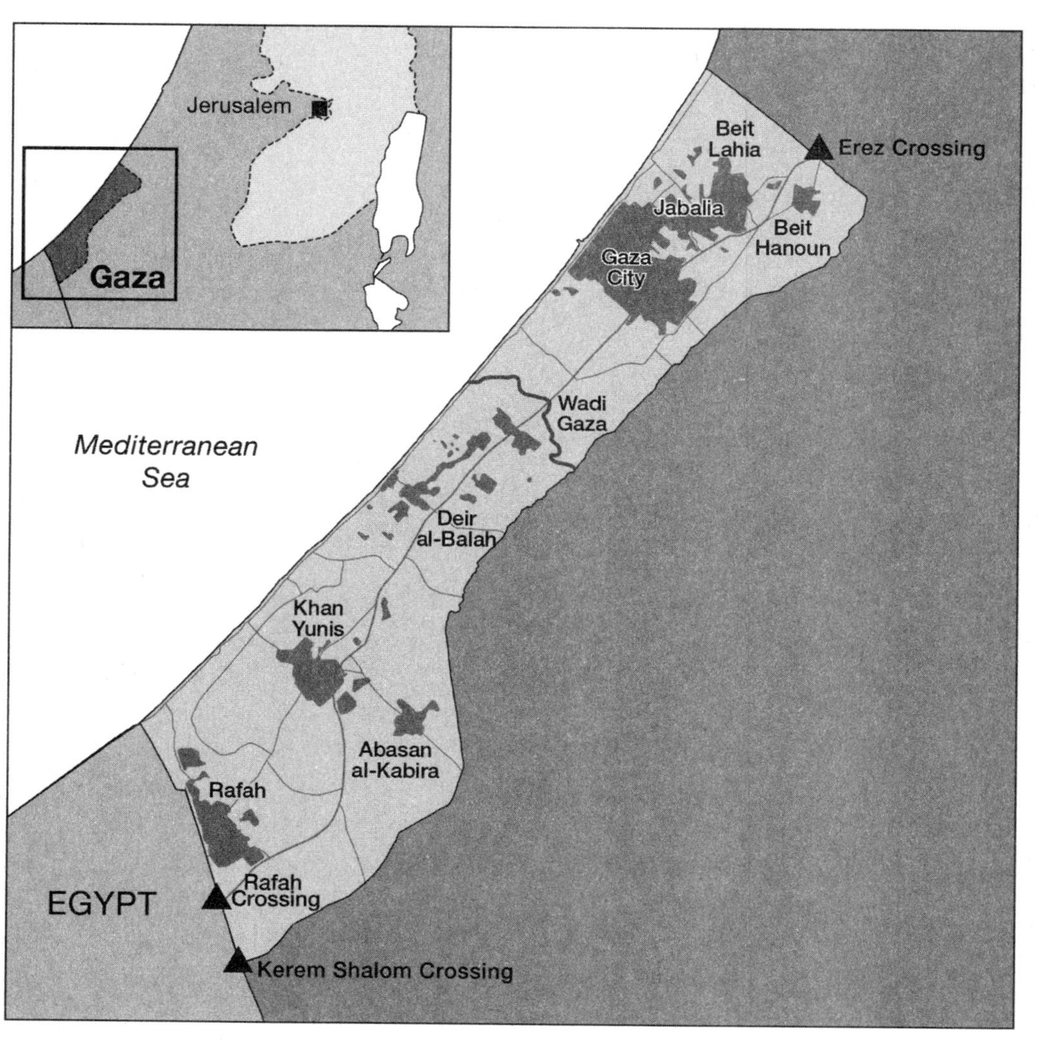
Jerusalem
Gaza
Beit
Lahia
Erez Crossing
Jabalia
Beit
Hanoun
Gaza
City
Wadi
Gaza
Mediterranean
Sea
Deir
al-Balah
Khan
Yunis
Abasan
al-Kabira
Rafah
Rafah
Crossing
EGYPT
Kerem Shalom Crossing

# *A Note on Translation*

"Translation is the most intimate act of reading." The definition comes from Gayatri Chakravorty Spivak, in a preface to her translation of eighteenth-century Bengali poetry. I didn't learn much in grad school, but I do remember at least one thing: it's a very bad idea to argue with Gayatri Spivak. So I won't. However, her insight, which has been seconded by scholars of translation everywhere, should really be understood as both a blessing and a curse. If translation is an intimate act, what then happens when a translator translates testimony from a witness to genocide?

Surely that translator is blessed to have been given a task of great urgency and lasting historical importance. Yet is this act of translation even possible? Can anyone from outside claim intimate knowledge of unspeakable crimes, especially someone with a privileged, sheltered perspective that never has had, and is unlikely ever to have, experience in any way approximating the lives that such an account must inevitably represent? Moreover, according to this definition, if translation is not intimate, it likely isn't translation at all, but instead simply betrayal—a false, distant, whitewashed image of the reality it purports to convey. And if the translation fails, won't readers necessarily fail as well? Or do readers inevitably fail anyway, if they fail to approximate the intimate act of translation?

Sami al-Ajrami's *The Keys to My House: A Gaza Diary* responds to each of these questions, and it does so with precision, compassion, and grace. Sami is a reporter who has worked for both Arab and

Israeli newspapers as well as a host of other news agencies, both regional and European. We may surely stipulate, without fear of contradiction, that the past two years in Gaza qualify as what Jalal Toufic calls a "surpassing disaster," and therefore we can also grant that the world will never fully know, that words can never adequately represent, the Palestinian experience—but that does not remove the obligation to report. What it does mean is that every reporter is also by definition a translator, and thus the weight on Sami al-Ajrami's shoulders is that of translation on every level: linguistic, cultural, even world-historical. In other words, the intimacy that Spivak intuits is a two-way street: we may read and understand as best we can, what Sami writes, but we should also remember that, like any good translator, al-Ajrami is in conversation with us.

This is no metaphor. Each day at 2:00 p.m., for the better part of six months (assuming that Sami could charge his phone, that the network wasn't down, and that other emergencies didn't take precedence), he would call to speak with Anna Lombardi and her colleagues in the foreign affairs office of Italy's *la Repubblica* newspaper. Each day he would recount what he had seen and heard and respond to questions about what he and his family, what his friends—what all of Gaza—was enduring, and his Italian colleagues would write it up. They would answer his questions too; the news went both ways. Readers need to appreciate the exceptional, collective origin of this narrative. Sami and Anna's intimate knowledge of their audience—of our language, of what we need to know—is the true gift within these pages.

Sami's war diary begins on October 13, 2023, with his family's exodus from their home in Gaza City. He then paints a brief, personal picture of the "Last Day of Peace," following it with a real-time account of the October 7 attack—given to us just as he and other Gazan journalists begin to piece together what is happening, and as they begin to reflect on what may happen next. From then on, we continue to follow—always in present tense, like a car driving through dense fog at night – Sami's war reports as well as his daily accounts of his family and friends, doing whatever they can to survive. The book ends just over six months later, with the author's departure from Gaza. Only at that point, in Egypt, did al-Ajrami and Lombardi meet for the first time, and they were able to continue the conversations that became this book.

As I write these words, despite the current "ceasefire" (during which hundreds of Palestinians have already been killed), Israel continues to prohibit the international press from witnessing and reporting freely on its actions in Gaza. Moreover, Israel, with outrageous hypocrisy, also discredits—not to mention targeting and murdering—Gazan reporters, while insuring that no other accounts will be written. For this reason, *The Keys to My House* is all the more precious. Despite the valiant efforts of a small number of translators, little magazines, and independent presses, for readers in English, stories like that of Sami al-Ajrami have remained largely untold and unheard. Given the power of the U.S., along with its role in aiding and abetting these massive war crimes, we should not be surprised that the story of Palestinian suffering—the ongoing Nakba—has not been a primary focus of Western news coverage.

After more than two years of genocidal slaughter, however, readers of this book may also wonder what will be gained by returning to an account of the war's first six months. Haven't events—the surpassing disaster being visited upon Gaza—long since eclipsed the undeniable horrors of this early period? For me, this question brings to mind the words of the Holocaust survivor Jean Améry, in what is arguably the most important essay ever written on torture. Améry observes that, *with the very first blow*, the victim of torture loses what he calls "trust in the world": "the certainty that the other, on the basis of written or unwritten social contracts, will spare me, and more precisely that they will respect my physical and thus also metaphysical existence." He further notes that, "with the first blow from a police officer's fist, against which there can be no resistance and which no helping hand will parry, a part of our life ends and can never be revived." What we realize in reading Sami al-Ajrami's Gazan diary is that the early months of the war already contained the seeds of everything to come.

To give a quick example: its first chapter from December 2024 begins simply, "Gaza City no longer exists." I happened to translate that passage in mid-September 2025, just after Israel had launched its final ground offensive on the city, and just after the UN commission of inquiry had announced its verdict that Israel had committed genocide in Gaza. During January 2025, Sami reports on an Israeli conference that gathered ex-settlers of Gaza for a discussion of how to recolonize the Strip. He comments,

> I continue to think that this must be Israel's real plan. In the North, entire villages have been flattened, the farmland has been devastated, and they've exploded all the buildings left standing after the bombing. They don't want to leave us anything to return to.

Should we have been surprised, then, by the news in mid-October 2025 that Israeli troops, prior to their "retreat," burned large sections of Gaza City, including the last functional component of its sanitation infrastructure, thus ensuring that city will remain uninhabitable, perhaps for years? The pages of this book not only foresee much of the year and a half since al-Ajrami's exile from his homeland, they also warn about what may still be coming.

From the war's earliest days, friends and family came daily to ask Sami for advice. Many of the most intimate moments in *The Keys to My House* relate stories about the small community of choice he helps assemble, a mutual aid organization of roughly sixty people with four families at its center. "Each week," he tells us, "by sacrificing something from our scant rations, we manage to organize a special meal and prepare a dessert or some other dish that breaks the monotony. Planning this activity quickly becomes our main goal and purpose; the dinners are a product of research and sacrifice, and we all participate." Given the horrors they hope to survive, and all the evidence of inhumanity in these pages, such moments are a salutary reminder that, to cite Svetlana Broz, there are also "good people in dark times."

Still, the demands placed on Sami must have occasionally been unbearable: in one instance, he advises family members where to move; after taking his suggestion and moving to a "safe area," they end up dying under the bombing anyway. On another occasion, he convinces a friend to leave his apartment and finds another place for him and his family to stay. This time, just a few hours after the family moves, their home is destroyed. While staying with friends of friends in Rafah, Sami describes how his work causes this small community to depend on him: "As a journalist, I have access to WhatsApp groups where I exchange information with my colleagues [...] and so, each night I become the evening news." As his readers, thus, we are simply another link in a collaborative chain that began in Gaza; each day, Sami distilled the essence of everything he learned, he reflected on and analyzed its content, then narrated these events for others. Somehow, with the help of Anna Lombardi, the book's straightforward, lucid prose manages to convey a reality that remains unimaginable, even, I imagine, for its witnesses.

As I finished this translation, a thought came to me, one that I suspect many readers will share. Should we ask Sami for an update? How are he and his daughters doing now, in the time since they left Gaza? What about the many friends and family members who we come to know in these pages? Are they safe? Have they even survived? What hopes do they have for their future? The more I thought about it, however, the more certain I was that we have no right to such questions. As readers, we would surely love a happy ending, and perhaps even tragedy would offer some form of closure. Yet Jean Améry gets this right too, when he cites Proust on this score: "'Nothing actually happens as we hope it will, nor as we fear it will.' But not because, as they say, it 'exceeds our ability to imagine' (it's not a quantitative question), but instead because it isn't imagination, but rather, reality."

To the extent we share the horror, the angst, the unbearable knowledge that anyone and everyone's survival today in Gaza still dangles on a thread, perhaps we do have some intimate sense of what Palestinians must be feeling.

*Jim Hicks*

*For my parents, for my daughters, for my entire family,*
*for the friends I've shared my darkest moments with,*
*and for all the people I love*

*Sami's breakfast nook.*

Two comfortable armchairs, under a wide window, a coffee table between them, an ashtray I put there. My days would begin in that spot, sipping coffee and listening to the news. After that, I'd smoke my first cigarette. That corner—now in ruins—is what I miss, more than anything else. I have it in a photo, which I look at every day.

# OCTOBER

## The Key to My House

**At dawn on October 13**, a week after the Hamas attack on Israel, I decide to abandon my home and take my family away. It's Friday, a day off for us. A few hours earlier, a friend who works for an international NGO called to tell me that the Israeli army was making strange phone calls to people living in the north of Gaza. They were picking numbers at random (and they would continue to do this throughout the conflict); a voice on the phone would repeat the same message: "Get out. The bombing is about to begin. We are coming." I don't doubt for a minute that this information is accurate. But how soon do we have to go? And where can we go to? I don't sleep that night. I pace to and fro in my barely three-room apartment, touching everything.

This isn't a rented apartment in some random condominium. The house was built literally stone by stone by my family. My parents, Mohamed and Aisha, eighty-seven and eighty-two years old, live on the ground floor. My brother Ahmed, who is fifty-five and the only one of us who, like Dad, drives a taxi, lives on the second floor with his wife and four kids. The third of eight children and the oldest boy, I live on the third floor with my two nineteen-year-old daughters, the twins Ruba and Bisan. On the top floor is my other brother, Hassan; he's forty-two, with a wife and five small children. He's the manager of Al-Quds Hospital, which is run by the Red Crescent, a Palestinian humanitarian agency, part of the International Red Cross network.

I realize how much every object that surrounds me tells a story. Representing moments of my life, each is connected to my family—Bedouins from the Negev Desert, with our origins in Beer Sheva, that great desert city occupied by the Israelis in 1948. After moving several times, Grandfather Hassan landed in Gaza in 1953, settling with his six children in a refugee camp in Jabalia. They lived in a tent that eventually got turned into a shack, and then finally into a house made of brick. I was born there, on February 14, 1967, on St. Valentine's Day—for us too, a day to celebrate love—in the tragic year of the Six-Day War, what we call the *Naksa,* or defeat. In this period, there was another exodus, and my entire clan, 400 families, came to Jabalia. We were so many that in 1972 the street was named after us: Ajrami Street. It was here, in 1991, that we built the house where we live.

We have always lived in Gaza; my entire life is stored within the walls of my home. The rooms are packed: souvenirs from places visited, gifts from friends, photos, my books, and a collection of colognes, my weakness. Along with my daughters' treasures.

At 5:00 AM I receive confirmation of my fears: on the Facebook page of Avichai Andrei, Arabic spokesperson for the Israeli army, an official declaration appears, requesting that all the Palestinians in the north evacuate to south of the Wadi Gaza nature reserve, into the center of the Gaza Strip. We'll be safe there, it states. "The ground invasion is about to begin."

Like every Palestinian in wartime, I'm ready. I gather documents—identity cards, passports, birth certificates, property records, and titles for the house—and wake my daughters and my parents, advising them to take only whatever is most important. We need to hurry; I want to leave as soon as possible. The girls don't complain. They pack their bags and have just one question: whether they can bring the violins they're learning to play. "No, only the essential," I reply. All five of us need to fit—plus our dog Milo and our cat Noga—in my red Opel Corsa. "Take some warm clothes," I advise. October has been warm, but winter is coming. When Ruba, in a near whisper—she's always the one who speaks, even for her sister—says,

"We're ready," we leave. I double-lock the door and put the keys in my pocket.

History is repeating itself, I think. Like my grandparents, who had to abandon their home and land, taking only their keys with them, hoping one day to claim their right to return, I too am going away, keys in my hand, already imagining I'll be able to return. "Don't look back," I whisper to the girls. We go downstairs to my parents'. My mother, wearing her usual Bedouin clothing, is confused. She doesn't want to leave this home; she has lived here for more than thirty years. I load the car and help my father, who is sick, to get in and fasten his seatbelt. We're all in place, but I hesitate anyway. I ask, for the umpteenth time, "Did we take everything?"

## *The Last Day of Peace*

**It's hard to imagine that** just a week ago (on October 6, another Friday, a day off to spend with family), we were carefree, even happy, I dare say. It had been a politically calm period. Convinced war wasn't about to break out again, in June I had bought a small farm at the northern border of the Strip. Five hundred square yards of cultivable land, in an area called Sudania, just over half a mile from the Israeli border. It was my dream: from there, the Mediterranean Sea was visible. I thought of building a house with a wide window to capture the view. I certainly didn't imagine this would be our last day of peace; I invited my brother Hassan and his family over, to show them the place.

The house still had to be built; for now, there was only the outline that I'd drawn on the ground. But I had already built myself a bathroom with a shower, so I could freshen up after working. I remember us speaking at length about practical things: where to place the new plants, how to construct an efficient irrigation system. On the orange trees that came with the land, the fruit was already almost ripe. A few days longer and we would have brought in our first harvest. My daughters were enjoying themselves, playing with their cousins: "If anyone touches them, they'll be sorry!" Our next-door neighbor, meanwhile, was planting strawberries. I asked him if we could pick some too; I knew how different the taste would be from the ones you buy at the market. We traded a few jokes. We ate, we joked, we worked. In sum, we spent a simple day together, a day of work and joy; we finished wiring the electrical service and hung lights, so we could stay late that evening.

On that warm and quiet night, we got back home at 10:00 PM. Since I wasn't sleepy, I stayed up talking with my brother in the kitchen until two. We didn't imagine the world we'd be in just a few hours later.

## *October 7, 2023*

I WAKE WITH A START from an extremely loud noise. The first light of dawn is coming through the window: it must be about six in the morning. The sound is terrifying, close enough that everything shakes. I run out to the balcony to look at what's happening, but I don't see anything. It's Saturday, the day of rest in Israel, and, what's more, it's Simchat Torah, the final day of the Sukkot holidays. I turn on my computer and scroll through the news. Everything there is from the previous day. Nothing on the Palestinian radio channels or Israeli TV either. However, the chat group for Gaza journalists—640 of us total—starts to show some activity. We're all asking each other what's happening, but no one knows anything. Until one of us remarks that he'd just seen a strange photo posted on Facebook by his neighbor—showing men from Hamas crossing the border.

The image shocks me. I too began to follow that profile: the man—later arrested and disappeared—is with militia members inside Israel, something unheard of. The more I look at his photos, the more I understand that something enormous is happening. For the people of Gaza, crossing that limit is unimaginable: the border is armed with sensors capable of firing automatically. It often happens when animals pass by; even some farmers have died when they got too close with their spades.

On social media I see disturbing images. Out of instinct, some of my colleagues have rushed to the spot with cameras, and they post what is happening live. For reacting so quickly, they will win the

Pulitzer Prize, but Israel will accuse them of being embedded with the terrorists, with prior notice about the events. A grievous insinuation, given that they were in fact the ones to show the world the enormity of this attack. I can't figure out why it is taking the Israelis so long to intervene, leaving the militias free to act. They attack for hours without impediment and as a result kill 1,200 people. No one intervenes until 10:30 AM. The more I get a sense of how serious this attack is, the more I realize how long and painful the response will be.

I don't go out before afternoon. In the streets, some are celebrating, believing that what has happened is payback, after suffering so many humiliations. Besides, the Israeli-Palestinian conflict in different periods has witnessed varied levels of fighting. But the last seventeen years have been the worst. After Hamas came to power, the Strip has been imprisoned within a tight blockade that has worn us to the breaking point. Unemployment, especially among the young, has reached unprecedented levels. The economy in Gaza has rapidly collapsed. Anger toward Israel has increased in a population that is frustrated and impoverished. The society has become more conservative, and many have joined ranks with the armed factions of Hamas or the Islamic Jihad. Therefore, the day after October 7, many people see the attack as payback, a demonstration that popular resistance alone isn't enough to end the occupation.

Others, however, are worried and ask me what I think. In our neighborhood, they call me the "political analyst" because I'm a journalist and I speak Hebrew well; I learned it on my own at twelve, when there were still Israeli colonists in Gaza, and I wanted to know what they were saying to each other. I bought a textbook with the title *Hebrew Without Teachers*, and I found out I had a talent for languages. In Tel Aviv during the '80s, I became fluent, studying English as well and working for a construction company.

That very linguistic competence, in 1999, allowed me to join the diplomatic corps of the Palestinian Authority as an interpreter and "analyst of Israeli affairs," working during the next five years for their Negotiations Affairs Department, then directed by Mahmoud

Abbas, the future Abu Mazen. When he became prime minister, I moved to the WAFA news agency, a Palestinian news and information service. Then Hamas came to power in 2007 and fired all the Palestinian Authority employees. I next began writing for the Israeli daily *Maariv.* (I imposed two conditions: I would never refer to the Israeli army as a "defense force" nor call the Palestinians "terrorists.") Soon, working with Israeli newspapers was also prohibited. I still managed to get by, working as a fixer, accompanying foreign journalists around Gaza. At that time, I became a correspondent for a variety of newspapers and news agencies, including the German *Berliner Zeitung* and the Italian *ANSA*.

That's why my neighbors came to me. They wanted help in understanding what was about to happen. "The response will be severe," I reasoned. "But I'll only be able to say more after the second month of the war." They became nervous. "Will the war really last two months?" they asked, incredulously. The longest war in Gaza had lasted "only" fifty-one days, and that was the limit of their imagination.

"It will last *at least* two months. This war isn't like the others."

## *The Wrath of Israel*

**Israel didn't keep us waiting** for a response. At sunfall on that same tragic day, bombs begin to drop on Gaza. They first strike the fourteen-story Watan Tower, the center hosting the area's internet service, taking out the entire network. A predictable move: Israel always starts up its wars where the last one left off, and the last war stopped short of bombing skyscrapers. The tallest buildings are thus its first target.

Next come the mosques: the mosque of Ali, near my house, falls, with its imam inside. The dead body of that short, taciturn man, who was affiliated with the Islamic Jihad, would only be found days later.

These are hours of turmoil. No one manages to sleep; fear and the incessant noise make it impossible: the rumble of airplanes, the din of bombs, the whoosh of missiles, the buzzing of drones, the screams of desperation. At 3:00 am, after a call from the army, someone in Gaza City sounds a new alarm, shouting from the loudspeakers of Al-Sousi Mosque, "Escape immediately!" A few moments later, an attack destroys the mosque along with a five-floor residential building nearby.

By dawn on October 8, the greater part of Gaza has already been flattened. The skyscrapers with major businesses. The commercial district. The universities. At first light, exhausted, terrorized men and women pour back out into the streets, anxious to gather provisions and barricade themselves at home, waiting for whatever comes next. Long lines form in front of bakeries, supermarkets, gas stations.

At noon, without warning, a building in Jabalia, the home of the Shekeian family, is targeted; apparently there are four hostages and some Hamas militants inside. The house faces the parking lot of the largest supermarket in the area, and in that moment, it is densely crowded. The first massacre. A wave of explosions shakes the earth, raising up a wall of dust and smoke, making it impossible to flee. A great number of us run to the scene, and when the thick fog dissipates, we find ourselves in front of a scene of horror. Blood and shredded bits of bodies have become one with the rubble from the destroyed buildings. On the ground lie fifty dead and 150 wounded. So many are children. Emergency teams arrive immediately. We stare somberly at their movements as they work to pull the survivors out of the debris. Everyone is asking why they bombed that specific house with so much force, destroying everything around it—wouldn't a precision strike have sufficed? What does Israel want: to rescue the hostages and defeat Hamas, or to destroy Gaza? I'm still asking myself that question.

During those same hours, a bit farther to the north, the village of Beit Hanoun is also attacked, barely four miles from the Israeli city of Sderot. In the first years of the 2000s, the militias launched their Qassam rockets on Israel from there. Not a surprising target. After the bombing, all its 50,000 inhabitants—mostly farmers—are forced to leave. They come en masse to Jabalia, an ex-refugee camp already overcrowded under normal conditions, a beehive of 170,000 people forced to live on top of each other. Women and children fill the streets and camp on the sidewalks while the heads of families look for lodging with family members or rentals. By the evening, there's no longer a single free apartment from Jabalia to Gaza City.

Meanwhile, on the chat groups used by various ministers of Gaza to communicate with journalists, the first sad statistic appears, a sort we will soon become accustomed to: in a single day, 600 dead, a third of them children; sixteen skyscrapers have been destroyed, along with more than one hundred houses and dozens of mosques. Corpses and rubble are everywhere. Israel even cuts off the supply of electricity. We're in the dark.

Still enthused after yesterday's attack, men from the armed branch of Hamas, the Izz al-Din al-Qassam brigades, launch rockets at Tel Aviv; they even send an ultimatum, to show that they are firmly in control. "If you continue the bombing, we will kill the hostages," they say, referring to the 242 people who were kidnapped and brought inside the Strip. This warning drops into the void.

## *Prewar Gaza*

**The Gaza Strip is a** patch of land twenty-five miles long with a width of six miles at its widest point. In October 2023, roughly 2.3 million people live here, 70 percent of whom are "refugees" who escaped from elsewhere. They live in eight different camps that over time have become cities.

A territory inhabited principally by Palestinians—until 1918 Gaza belongs to the Ottoman Empire. It later becomes a British protectorate, and then, at the end of the Second World War, is given to Egypt by the United Nations, in anticipation of the formation of a Palestinian state. Israel, however, takes over the land in 1967, during the Six-Day War, when it defeats the Egyptians, Syrians, and Jordanians, increasing its territory from 13,000 to 63,000 square miles.

In the years that follow, roughly 8,000 Jewish settlers move into Gaza; they take possession of 40 percent of the land and control its water resources. Illegally, according to the international community. They leave in 2005, cleared out by the Israeli government within the scope of a long, painstaking process that history remembers as the "Plan for Unilateral Disengagement." Protecting its occupation costs Israel too much, especially after the two uprisings known as the First Intifada (1987–1993) and the Second Intifada (2000–2005).

The Palestinian Authority takes control of the Strip, but it is quickly challenged by Hamas, the Islamist movement founded as a local branch of the Muslim Brotherhood in 1987 by Ahmed

Yassin. Rivals of Yasser Arafat, the then Palestinian leader, its leaders had already gained recognition during the 90s with their kamikaze attacks aimed at blocking the Oslo Accords. In the parliamentary elections of 2006, they take over in Gaza, using extremism to master the difficult situation in the Strip. A brief civil war follows against those faithful to Mahmoud Abbas, who has just been elected president; Hamas is accused of having hatched some sort of coup. Hamas wins and remains in power until the present, strengthened by the isolation imposed by Israel, which separates Gaza off from the rest of the world. The blockade transforms the Strip into what Human Rights Watch defines as an "open-air prison," ensnaring its people within fences and barriers constantly surveilled by CCTV and drones. The population is even forced to report births and deaths to the Israeli state registry, as well as any imported merchandise.

In the Strip, there is also another faction: the Islamic Jihad. Founded in 1981 by Fathi Shaqaqi and Abd Al Aziz Awda, it again comes out of the Muslim Brotherhood, the Egyptian group that was spreading its roots into Palestine during this period. Influenced by the teaching of Ayatollah Khomeini, it has ties with Iran. Hamas and Jihad are sometimes allies, more often rivals.

# *A Safe Place*

**On the second day of** the war, it's late already when I get a call from my dear friend, Fatma Ashour, a forty-year-old lawyer and activist for the rights of women, well known in Gaza for her defense of dissidents and journalists who get in trouble with the local authorities. Her apartment is on the eighth floor of a residential building in central Gaza City; she tells me that it never stops shaking. "I'm going to my sister's. She lives in a low-rise building, and I'll feel safer." She's the first of my closest friends to leave her home. Her sister lives near the Islamic university; within a few hours, the Israeli army orders them to evacuate, announcing new rounds of bombing. "Now where do we go?" she asks me, in a second phone call.

With each war, this is how things go: whoever has the means tries to avoid the bombs by renting a more secure refuge elsewhere, or by escaping abroad. This last option is never easy; you need both money and connections. Up till now, the rich have always been the first to get out, finding safety in Egypt with family, but this time it's different. During the first hours of the war, Israeli bombardments surround the checkpoint near the Rafah crossing, the southernmost part of the Strip bordering on Egypt: the passage is immediately blocked with cement barricades.

Incredulous, many Gazans go there anyway, and remain there, waiting. One is my friend, Fadi Ali, who works for an NGO. He was living in Gaza City with his family, in a spacious apartment in the upscale neighborhood of Rimal, proud of his window with a sea view.

He told me by phone, "I was hoping that the border would be open, and I headed towards Rafah, but I was caught up in the bombing. So I changed plans and took the family to my father's in Khan Yunis. With a sigh, he tells me that his sea view is no more: "Now the scene below is terrible. The green zones are gone; everywhere you see just rubble and clouds of smoke. The government offices, the trendy restaurants, the stores, everything we saw from our window has been destroyed. And my kids saw that slaughterhouse with their own eyes. They'll be traumatized by it forever." Immediately after the first bombs fell, he put his family on the list for "coordination," which is what we call the system that allows travel without visas from Gaza to Egypt—an agreement from 2007 to let cross, along with foreign passport holders, people who need to travel abroad for business, study, or medical care.

There's also another way. Those with the means to do so contact specific travel agencies whose offers include, for a hefty fee, paperwork for visa procedures and transport to Cairo. Within the first hours of the war, requests made to those agencies reach enormous numbers. Prices go sky-high. But to no avail; the border is closed.

## *Rich and Poor*

**Whoever doesn't manage to snap** up one of the best sites of refuge goes to look for shelter in one of the schools run by UNRWA (the United Nations Relief and Works Agency for Palestinian Refugees in the Near East), founded at the end of the war in 1948. We feel protected under the UN banner, and for this reason, taking refuge within the premises of UNRWA-run organizations has been a constant throughout each of our wars. Financed by voluntary donations from UN-member states, UNRWA has always worked to maintain a dignified quality of life within the difficult environment of our refugee camps, managing the essential services: education, health and hygiene, social and humanitarian support. In Gaza, they've opened 183 schools where 9,443 teachers teach. They manage twenty-two clinics, where a thousand doctors are employed, as well as senior centers, playgrounds, and even the waste disposal facility. Over time, they've given food, shelter, and emergency loans to refugees exhausted by the embargo, which includes 70 percent of the population of Gaza—nearly 1,300,000 people. With 13,000 people on its payroll, UNRWA is the largest employer in the Strip.

Among the first to seek shelter in one of their buildings are fourteen members of the Jendeya family, who have been forced to leave their home in Shuja'iyya and take refuge at Tunis Elementary School, in the Tel al-Hawa neighborhood of Gaza City. They are assigned an entire schoolroom, but the family, unused to forced intimacy between men and women, decides to have the women and children sleep inside; the men find room in the hallways or outside. Penniless, they depend on aid even for their meals.

In the same school, the next night, the four members of Kareem Abu Shala's family also arrive, after escaping a violent assault. Kareem, a sturdy thirty-six-year-old man, tells me how he walked in the dark, pierced by flashes of shellfire, through the rubble and broken glass of the Ali Mosque, holding his five-year-old child by one hand with the other carrying a cage with five precious birds he cared about deeply. Behind him was his wife with their baby, just a few months old, in her arms.

"I didn't think that the fighter jets would attack our area, which is usually safe. When we left, we didn't have even enough time to close the door." He is angry. "No one gave us any warning. Not the interior minister, not the Department of Health. We're left completely on our own, and we have to figure everything out for ourselves." In fact, until now the only information given by the authorities consists of the emergency numbers for hospitals and fire stations, along with instructions for identifying the safest part of a house to shelter in during bombardments.

In short order, the situation in the schools worsens. Within just a few days, seven thousand people end up in that single building. Each classroom eventually has to house up to six families, around one hundred people. Privacy and services are lacking. Everyone has to share the small number of bathrooms. Living spaces are separated laboriously by hanging curtains on clotheslines.

Meanwhile, another uncontrollable factor is added to the fear and chaos. As a form of revenge, some Israelis are sending messages to the residents of Gaza from unlisted numbers. They impersonate the military and order evacuations, saying that the homes of those people are about to be bombed. It only takes one message for entire neighborhoods to be emptied. This panic adds to the awful news from Israeli media: government leaders speak about "razing Gaza to the ground," "sealing off the borders," "starving the citizens to death," and "launching massive military operations." Which is in fact about to happen.

## *The Great Thirst*

**On the fifth day of** bombing, after 300,000 of its soldiers have already been deployed at the border, Israel suspends the supply of all vital resources to the entire Strip. Beginning with water, which here has always served as a weapon of war. Brian Lander, Deputy Director of Emergencies for the World Food Program, is the first to sound the alarm internationally: "Fuel, water, and electricity are in limited supply. Bakeries have almost no flour left, shelters are under assault. Food and water are being rationed and will soon run out."

As soon as the frequency of bombing lessens, the residents of Gaza take the opportunity to go out with the large yellow five-gallon fuel cans always found in every home. They go in search of tank trucks full of potable water, hoping to fill them with a quantity that will last, on average, for a day. Ahmed Eita, twenty-six years old, is the eldest of five children, and he is saddled with the unrewarding job of stocking up. I meet him in the crowded streets of Jabalia while, waiting for the tankers, he is bargaining with vegetable vendors in their donkey-drawn carts.

"I'm only buying what we need for today," he says. "Without electricity, you can't keep anything fresh. We don't waste water, even to do laundry." In front of us, there's an enormous pile of trash, most of it broken glass, from the repeated aerial attacks. "If the war lasts more than a week, we'll die anyway," Ahmed sighs.

Water wells and desalinators are still working, running on power from gas-fueled generators. To reduce usage, they're running only four hours a day, rather than the usual twelve. Without fuel, the waterworks won't be able to keep up with the demand for long. According to Samer Abdeljaber, Palestinian Director of the World Food Program, the situation is devasting: "Supplies of gas, water, and electricity will soon run out."

Water supply in Gaza was already a problem. There is only one source that provides fresh water to the Strip: a coastal aquifer that extends from the north of Israel to the Sinai Peninsula in northern Egypt. It has been under Israel's control since the beginning of the occupation. According to a UN study, 66 percent of the water is taken by Israel, 23 percent by Gaza, and 11 percent by Egypt. Over time, however, overuse has caused its level to drop too much, allowing it to become contaminated with sea water. Deep wells dug by Israel have recently caused reserves to drop further. A study done in 2020 concluded that 97 percent of the water is no longer potable due to high salinity and contamination with wastewater.

For this reason, each neighborhood has a well of non-potable water, supplied to local residents only twice a day, which they conserve through various complex procedures. To many Gazan households, electricity is in fact delivered only in eight-hour shifts. In practice, if one block is illuminated, the next one is in the dark. When there is electricity, everyone knows that they'll have running water for two hours. To conserve as much as possible, each household runs its own electric pump to fill its rooftop cistern.

Since the settlers retreated eighteen years ago, there has no longer been drinkable running water. Private businesses desalinate some amount of water and then resell it on demand, delivering it in tank trucks. Before the war, the average daily water use per capita in Gaza was 86.6 liters, of which only 26.8 were potable, well under the 100 liters per day established as a basic necessity by the World Health Organization.

## *Deir al-Balah*

**Exactly a week has passed** since the start of the war. In the car with my parents and daughters, ready to flee, I sum up out loud everything we've packed. We have my father's medicines, but my mother doesn't have any warm clothing. Incredulous, she asks me twice, "Do you really think that's necessary?" She can't accept the idea that she won't be going home soon. Finally, I convince her. She gets out of the car, goes inside, and grabs her heavy coats and scarves. It's nearly 7:00 AM and the neighbors, who are all up by now, surround our car, skeptical and sarcastic. "Why are you leaving?" they ask. They trust me and know that I follow the news. But they still don't realize.

"Scaredy cat!" one of them kids me. I respond, "Whoever doesn't leave now will leave naked." He himself will remind me what I told him, months later in Rafah. "I didn't leave in time, and, as you said, I had to leave naked. I couldn't take a single thing with me." I'm the first in the neighborhood to leave. My brother Hassan packs his bags soon after. "I only understood how serious the situation was when I saw you leave," he will later admit. For many, going away is difficult. "Better to die in your own home," the neighbors say, shaking their heads, not understanding the enormity of their words. I start the motor and depart. To where, I don't yet know. An hour later I'm south of Wadi Gaza, in the area designated as safe by Israel.

At first, I have a vague idea that we should aim for Rafah, where we have relatives. I call them while driving, but I'm immediately disabused of that notion: they're also on their way to the center of the Strip, and the bombing has also targeted the area where they live. Then I have a sudden inspiration. For years, my sister Sanaa and her family have been living in Saudi Arabia. Her husband has done well there, enough to have built a fancy cottage for them in Zawaida, near Deir al-Balah, where they spend their summer vacations. They call it, grandiosely, their "chalet." I call and ask point blank if we can stay there. They agree and set up a meeting with their custodian, who has the keys. It's a perfect arrangement: a lot of space and a view of the sea. The cottage has two floors, each with over 155 square yards; there is an enormous living room, five bedrooms, three bathrooms, and a huge deck. In their yard, which measures over six hundred square yards, they have a swimming pool, half-full of rainwater. In the days to come, we'll bathe in it. I get my parents settled and then call other relatives: my brothers and sisters, my uncles, aunts, and cousins. "There's room for everyone," I assure them.

In the hours that follow, so many arrive that, within a few days, we're too many even for that enormous villa—three hundred people. In customary fashion, the women are allowed to sleep inside whereas we men settle in outside, our cars or on the lawn. Only my brother Hassan decides to take shelter elsewhere; his employer, the Red Crescent, offers him lodging in its compound at Khan Yunis, where he can continue to work. He accepts, bringing his family there.

We get organized, dividing up duties, just as every family does everywhere. The key daily mission is to find enough to eat for a single meal, which serves as both lunch and dinner. To tell the truth, no one goes out willingly; although getting along is a strain, we are afraid that if we split up, we'll be separated forever. From the age of ten and up, all the boys are given small carts made of fruit crates mounted on wheels and told to make water runs; they drag the carts around for miles. The women stand in line for bread. Teenagers are tasked with finding canned food on the black market. Young girls stay home to take care of the infants and seniors, often by showing them episodes from TV series and music videos that they have stored on their phones.

We men go off instead looking for the little gas that's left, at prices that by now have gone crazy; gas is needed for the small amount of electricity that powers water pumps and desalinators as well as our radios—so we can find out what's happening. And recharge our phones, of course. We only turn the phones on during specific times, trying to quell as best we can our sense of isolation during the hours they're off. The days are labor-intensive, and they finish early. After we eat, we tell each other stories, recalling recent memories: last summer, someone's birthday, a party. At dusk we go to sleep. Or at least we try to.

*At the Al-Aqsa Hospital in Deir al-Balah.*

Bombs are also falling on the Salah al-Din Road, one of two streets that cross the whole zone declared by Israel as a safe area. Seventy people die and hundreds are wounded, so many that the Israeli army is obliged to specify that "travel is assured between 10:00 AM and 4:00 PM." People are acting in absolute uncertainty, hoping they make the right choices. From the window of our "chalet," I see them going down "the coast road," Al Rashid Street; it's longer but believed to be safer after the other road was bombed.

Thousands of people loaded down with whatever they manage to pack: mattresses, blankets, the increasingly rare crates of bottled

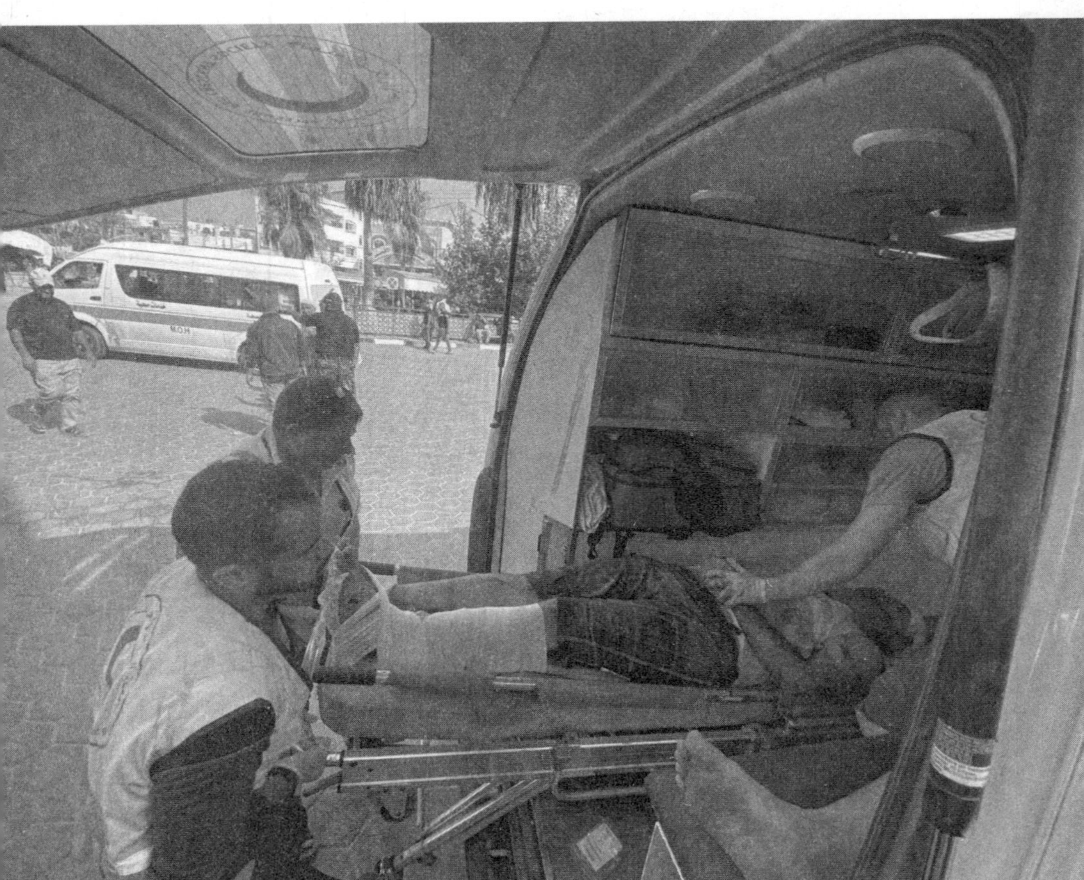

*Another deadly day at Al-Aqsa Hospital.*

water, pets, propane tanks. Tied down, in the best-case scenario, on top of cars—and bikes, and countless donkey carts. The donkey is now the principal means of transport for our wretched lives. Efficient and economical, for its endurance and for the small amount of food it needs and finds on its own, maybe by rummaging through garbage. In short order, the asking price for a donkey also goes up.

## *The Mukhtar*

**I'M STANDING AT THE WINDOW** when I get a phone call. It's Ayed al-Ajrami, a contractor and distant cousin of mine, but above all mukhtar of the entire al-Ajrami clan, with its multitudes in Gaza. An important tribal role: he heads a cabinet with nineteen advisors—all distant relatives—that manages problems facing our extended family. They take care of the most needy, for example, helping widows or paying school fees for talented but impoverished youth. Though we are on excellent terms, receiving a call from him is always an honor. "Explain what's happening," he says. "What's the best course of action?" I advise him to leave. He listens to me and immediately orders all his relatives to move to the center of the Strip. For his family, he rents a triple-decker house in Deir al-Balah. Very soon, however, I will regret my advice.

Only two days later, on October 15, bombs begin to fall even in the so-called safe zone below Wadi Gaza. And even the sleepy city of Deir al-Balah is hit. Israel justifies its actions: "Hamas soldiers are hiding there." By now it's clear: to kill even one member of Hamas, Israel will destroy everything in the area. Many innocent civilians are killed. Fourteen are from my family, including Ayed's entire family—and I was the one who suggested they come here.

I identify their bodies at Al-Aqsa Hospital, where I had rushed to report on the news, and I am devastated. Their bodies are laid out under a large tent outside the main building. Each time an ambulance arrives the same sad ritual repeats. Family members arrive

*October, 2023. Fourteen members of the Ajrami family are killed.*

to see if their relatives are among the dead. If they don't find them, they run to the ER, thanking God out loud. Yet the situation they find there is hardly reassuring. A few exhausted doctors do their best to keep the severely wounded alive. You hear irrepressible moans and screams of pain. There's not enough power to refrigerate and preserve the bodies. Unable to give them any better funeral, we pray quickly in front of the remains, which have since been wrapped in shrouds. We load them onto a small, open-bed rental truck and bring them to the local cemetery, which is already more than full. We are forced to dig between other tombs and bury our loved ones there, each on top of the others.

There's not much time to mourn the dead. The situation for the living is desperate: there's no more water, so we must boil and reboil water we've used already, then use it again. We ration it. Each of us has less than a liter and a half to do everything: drink, wash, go to the toilet. We establish rigid rules. We drink only at specific times, and mothers must supervise what babies drink, difficult as it is to explain why they have to wait between one sip and the next.

Food becomes scarce. To buy bread you have to wait hours in line. And when your turn comes, you barely get enough to sustain yourself for another day. In the mornings, we drink tea, which there is plenty of: it's our breakfast, and we drink it without sugar, that goes without saying. By noon we're suffering from cramps, but we do everything possible to postpone lunch until late afternoon, so that we don't suffer from hunger during the night. We eat rice and canned meat or beans—enough to survive, though not enough to feel full. Around the table, however, the tension is finally broken. During meals, at least, we try to laugh, making fun of that day's difficulties.

## *People in the North*

**Roughly 600,000 people, a third** of the population of Gaza, are still in the North. They stay there above all out of terror: they fear a new Nakba, or "catastrophe," which is our name for the forced exodus of 1948, when after fighting the Israelis, the Palestinians were forced to flee and their homes were occupied. "If we leave, our homes will be taken away too," they say, torn between the risk of dying crushed under the rubble of their own homes and that of losing everything and having to resign themselves to an uncertain future in a refugee wasteland for years to come.

The market in the refugee camp of Jabalia is bombed repeatedly, as are a number of still functional bakeries in Gaza City. Families are forced to seek new shelter repeatedly—four times, or five. With the residential areas downtown reduced to rubble, these quests push them more and more toward the suburbs, carrying minimal bags on the back, compelled to react quickly. Soon even the support services disappear. There's no longer any way to search for potential survivors—doomed to die slow, atrocious deaths, their bodies left to rot. Even the Al-Zahraa neighborhood is destroyed. Thirty densely inhabited apartment buildings, completely flattened. The inhabitants believed they'd be safe, because it had always been a peaceful area. Instead, they have to leave in a hurry, finding their way through darkened streets with no electricity. Yes, Israel does give its usual warning, randomly calling someone's cell phone, but at 9:00 PM, when many people are already sleeping. The bombs begin to fall right on time, a half hour later, and they continue without pause until morning.

Life in the North is quickly transformed into constant terror. And after the first week, people begin to realize the gravity of the choice they've made. Much more than in the South, they suffer from hunger and thirst, compelled to gather dirty water out of bomb craters, from broken pipes that once connected the water system to subterranean aquifers. As a result, scabies and cholera begin to spread. No one has work; they get by through black-market bartering, or, at great risk, by smuggling something in from the South. Only at the hospitals—all at their breaking points—is work not lacking. Doctors and nurses would like to find safety, but instead they're forced to work twenty hours a day, long shifts with no days off, and sleep on hospital stretchers.

Israel threatens Al-Quds Hospital, where my brother works, in the residential neighborhood of Tel al-Hawa, right in the center of Gaza City. It is privately run, managed by the Red Crescent, and was already bombed in 2009, then reconstructed with funding from Qatar and France. Inside there are 400 severe medical cases and 12,000 refugees. They sleep on the roof, in the hallways, on the stairs—convinced that the Israelis will spare medical facilities. There are relatives who don't want to abandon their children, husbands and wives, parents, siblings who are sick and defenseless. No ultimatum will convince them: "We won't go until you take everyone here somewhere safe." Not even the doctors leave; they can't abandon dangerously ill patients, and the patients can't be taken elsewhere because there aren't enough ambulances. Yet in the meantime the bombing by the army comes closer and closer to the medical facility, striking neighboring buildings with the goal of chasing everyone out. They want to get inside the hospitals at all costs, convinced that militants are hiding there. Physicians for Human Rights Israel, a medical NGO, attempts to help the doctors and patients by presenting a petition at the Israeli Supreme Court, explaining why, in such conditions, the hospital cannot be evacuated. They obtain a positive response and a temporary suspension of military operations.

Meanwhile, however, even the area around Al-Shifa Hospital is hit. Al-Shifa is the central and largest hospital of the entire Strip; it was built in a former British barracks at Rimal and transformed into a sanatorium in 1946. Full to overflowing with severe cases, many of its patients are hooked up to ICU therapies.

Even the people who look for shelter in the Church of Saint Porphyrius—an orthodox church that dates back to the fifth century, the oldest in Gaza—end up regretting their decision. It is bombed, despite the fact that it welcomed in only a small community of 400 congregants. Eighteen of them die, including a twenty-six-year-old employee of Caritas, her husband, and infant daughter.

*Attack on the Church of Saint Porphyrius*

The Orthodox Patriarch of Jerusalem thunders, "Targeting churches and their organizations, together with shelters that protect innocent civilians, is a war crime. It cannot be ignored."

The 160,000 people sheltering in the fifty-seven schools run by UNRWA in northern Gaza are left entirely on their own. After losing twenty-nine workers in the bombing, the agency decides to transfer all its personnel to the South and states clearly to everyone, "You need to leave. The United Nations is no longer able to guarantee your safety or offer assistance." Nonetheless, many people remain. They don't know where else to go.

Finding a safe place is harder and harder. In the Strip, bombs are falling everywhere. They kill dozens in Al-Shati refugee camp in the North. And a hundred or so in the Nuseirat market, targeted on two occasions when it was packed with people searching for food, people that newscasts refer to, horrifically, as "collateral damage." The target of this latest raid is a building that is unfortunately close to Abu Dallal, the largest supermarket in Gaza, which in its turn is also reduced to rubble. By now it is clear: when the army has a target it will not hesitate to turn an entire neighborhood to dust. And this causes panic in the entire, exhausted population, including those who have obeyed the ultimatum of October 13, where the area below Wadi Gaza was declared a safe zone. As a result, everyone in the North wants to move to the South. And vice versa, the evacuees want to return home. By this point, however, moving at all has become difficult, and, due to the lack of gas, extremely expensive. Whoever has any is saving it, as a cautionary measure. Or so that prices will rise. The few taxis still circulating ask for astronomical fares: 1,000 shekels, about 250 dollars, for a fifteen-to-eighteen-mile trip.

## *Return to Gaza City*

**On the evening of October 17**, a massacre is perpetrated in a place no one could have expected: Al-Ahli Hospital, run by the Episcopal Church of Jerusalem—a location where no armed militants could have been, since the church leaders would never have allowed it. When I get there, the next morning, the scene is desolate. The lawn has been sprayed with blood, and bits of body parts are everywhere. In one of the crumpled cars, I glimpse a foot still wearing a shoe, cut cleanly off from who knows which body, one of the many that pious hands have vainly been trying to reassemble. Sobbing men and women wander about, seeking the remains of their loved ones. I meet a particularly distraught child. He is eight years old, and through his tears he tells me the sad tale of his family, entirely wiped out—thirty dead in total. Sadly, it isn't surprising that each bombing destroys entire families. In times of war, Gazan families always unite in a single spot; they share their meager rations of food and water, their blankets, and their fate. Ready to die together.

Israel and Hamas accuse each other of having provoked the massacre. In the days that follow, Al-Jazeera will report that the massacre was caused by bombing carried out by the Israeli army (which in that very moment was hitting three other nearby locations), basing their conclusions on videos showing the skies overhead. A month later, however, a Human Rights Watch investigation will propose an alternative explanation, based on ground-level footage. According to analysts from the NGO, a failed rocket launch by the militants caused all these deaths: "We have identified parts of a weapon that is incompatible with those used by the Israeli forces."

What is certain is that the hospital parking lot and a nearby park were hit; both were extremely crowded, since it was already dark and many people were sleeping, camped out on the lawn or in their cars. The attack caused the medical staff, who continued to work nonstop, to evacuate all civilians.

My trip back to Gaza City, en route to the hospital, was surprising. The streets were empty. Piled up along the roadside, however, were dozens of burned-out cars, along with mountains of garbage that no one removes anymore, because there's no gas in the garbage trucks.

I cross entire neighborhoods in ruin, where I no longer recognize anything. Everywhere is an overpowering stench of corpses abandoned under the rubble; there isn't even enough gas for the three backhoes still able to move heavy debris. The heat causes the remains of those poor souls to decompose rapidly, polluting the soil and attracting all sorts of animals—rats, beetles, crows, and who knows what else. In any case, burying the dead has become difficult even for those left at the morgues. There's no fuel to get them to cemeteries. If no one claims them, they simply pile up in refrigerator trucks left—no longer running—in the parking lots. There's no diesel for them either.

At Al-Quds Hospital the medical staff operates in the dark, because their last generator is running practically on fumes, so overloaded that it needs constant attention. They use it for the intensive care unit, the only ward that still has lights; they've brought refrigerators with the blood supply and other vital medicine there, along with neonatal incubators and respirators for patients unable to breathe on their own.

I should admit it. Besides my obligations as a journalist and the hospital massacre, I have another reason for coming north again. Last night, in fact, we used up the last propane tank for our stove. We were debating vociferously where we might find a replacement when my mother interrupted and said, "There's one hidden in my bedroom." We all turn toward her in disbelief: people are offering to risk their lives to find us one, when she has a spare hidden in Jabalia! I decide to brave the risky trip back there to retrieve it. I stop by the hospital so I can write my article, and then I head for Jabalia. I sneak through the door of my parents' apartment; the neighborhood is deserted, and I feel like a thief in my own home, a truly weird sensation. I'm tempted to climb the two flights of stairs to visit my apartment as well, but I decide not to. I can't stay long, and I'd already said my goodbyes; given what time it is, the trip back will be even more dangerous. I find the propane tank and leave.

On the way back, I pass through Zeitoun. It's the only neighborhood where life seems to continue. There are people in the streets, stores open, even a bakery still churning out bread. People are lining up to charge their phones by attaching them to car batteries; they tell me that they're using them not for phone calls, but to have light in their homes after dark. They tell me repeatedly that they're not planning to leave. "The war will end soon," they insist. The words of President Biden, who has rushed to Israel, give them hope. He has extracted a promise that the Rafah crossing will be opened to humanitarian aid. "A truce will be next," they say. "The war will end soon."

## *The Rafah Crossing*

THE NEWS THAT THE RAFAH crossing is about to reopen spreads quickly throughout the entire Strip. It's even scheduled: between 9:00 AM and 5:00 PM, so that aid can come in and those with foreign passports can leave. "Lucky" Palestinians, who get going quickly and make it to the area, are hoping they'll be able to leave. They set up camp in the least bad location they can find, under a boiling sun. In the early hours of the morning, I join them. The checkpoint is still closed, with the same cement blocks that have been there since October 7. Within a few hours, the chaos becomes indescribable. Everywhere men are shouting; exhausted women have hungry, crying children in their arms or hanging onto their skirts. They fight over nothing: a slight bit of shade, a glance too many at the older daughters, one foot stepping on another. And to make tempers worse, the constant rumble of nearby artillery. They realize they're in danger, out in the open, but they're too desperate to go anywhere else. The crossing might open at any minute and then close again soon after, for whatever reason. They need to rise to the occasion; it might happen soon.

Staff from UNRWA and the Palestinian Red Crescent are also waiting, ready to receive incoming aid. By this point, they are the only organizations with warehouses big enough to store the supplies, the only ones with the logistical plans and the capacity to manage the distribution. The last who are still active and organized, unlike the other NGOs, with their personnel scattered or lost.

Hours pass, but the crossing remains closed. According to the news reports, Israel is refusing to grant safe passage; it wants its military to certify that only foreign passport holders are allowed to leave. Negotiations are being held, however, to determine who will receive the aid supplies; the army is obsessed by the idea that some of it will end up with Hamas. And they also use aid as an instrument to increase pressure on the Gazan population.

One day passes, then another. Palestinians with dual citizenship begin to lose hope. Staying out in the open is risky and exhausting, even more so now that radio broadcasts speak only about the negotiations over aid, not about letting the "foreigners" leave. Rafah empties out. Gone too are the security personnel and government officials who normally supervise the border; it has become too dangerous to work there. The city is deserted, with only one café still open. Inside I meet all five of its customers, the Palestinian staff of a Norwegian NGO. They really don't want to leave; they're afraid to lose their chance for salvation.

The logjam finally breaks at 10:30 AM on October 21, a Saturday. The border reopens for the first time since the day of the attack. Twenty trucks, blowing their horns, enter from the Sinai in Egypt, full of basic necessities given by allied countries. Above all there are canned goods (tuna, meat, and grains) and bottled potable water, which had been impossible to find, as well as medicine and medical equipment crucial for bringing hospitals back from the brink. Israel, however, has prohibited the importation of flour, despite the lack of it by now everywhere. Fuel is also prohibited, even though it is essential to run Gaza's indispensable generators. "The militants use it to fire rockets" is the official explanation. Another tall tale, woven to augment the collective suffering of civilians.

The aid is consigned to the Red Crescent officials and UNRWA staff. They carry everything across on thirty small trucks, then storing one part in Rafah—the border city with its 245,000 residents—and sending another to Khan Yunis, where the population of 350,000 has been doubled with refugees from the North. A third portion arrives to Deir al-Balah, the town with 87,000 inhabitants where I and my family are staying, not far from the Red Crescent warehouses.

According to the hard-earned agreement, these two organizations will be responsible for managing the aid distribution; they will follow a specified plan presupposing that its only beneficiaries will be populations and hospitals in the South. Provisions will not be allowed to go north of Wadi Gaza. If transport vehicles attempt to reach Gaza City, the army warns, they will be attacked and destroyed. And, in fact, each movement of the convoy is monitored by drones. We hear them buzzing in the air above, intent on assuring that all the conditions are met.

It seems that the negotiations over logistics will themselves slow matters down. Another 140 trucks loaded with supplies are waiting outside the borders of Gaza. Tedros Adhanom

Ghebreyesus, Director-General of the World Health Organization, put it clearly: "To meet the urgent health crisis in Gaza, the safe passage of additional convoys is necessary." Martin Griffiths, Coordinator of Emergency Aid for the United Nations, describes it as "insufficient amounts of aid, a drop in the bucket." Before the crisis began, an average of 450 truckloads per day were delivered to the Strip; this first delivery represents just three percent of what's needed. The 44,000 bottles of water delivered by UNICEF are fundamental, yet they are barely sufficient for the needs of 22,000 people during a single day. "With a million children at risk, water is a matter of life and death," says Catherine Russell, director of the United Nations Children Fund, in a radio interview. The provisions that do arrive are meager and often misplaced. Rice and lentils are sent to areas where there is no water or fuel to cook them.

The frustration is palpable. The aid isn't enough, and above all the ceasefire that we hoped would accompany it is lacking. Among the disappointed are the roughly one hundred families with dual passports who arrived at the crossing early that morning, without being summoned, in the hopes that they would be allowed to cross. I hear the heads of these families on the phone, crying and shouting with officials from their respective embassies, begging them to do more.

There is one bit of good news. Since the much-needed shipment of flour was not delivered, UNRWA announces its decision to use up its stockpile, distributing for free what it has left in its warehouses to sixteen bakeries in the South. As such, for a few days, we manage to find more bread, and we pay less for it, four shekels—about one dollar—for fifty pieces of pita bread. This was the pre-war price, rather than the eight shekels it had become. The endless lines that families had been enduring daily begin to shorten. And our stomachs fill up a bit at last.

Life, however, remains difficult. Gaza was already one of the most densely populated places on the planet before the war, and the evacuation southward of more than a million people has quickly overpopulated this narrow patch of land. In homes, tents, and shelters, dozens of people are forced to live literally one on top of another. Thirty or forty people sleep together in a single room. It's difficult to describe the heat or the odor of bodies that never have sufficient water for bathing. And the constant crying of children who are forced to stay entire days inside, anxious, with no one able to explain what is happening, since even the adults have trouble understanding it. Squabbles continue to break out over a sip of water or an extra morsel of bread. Also the moans of the sick: without potable water, cases of diarrhea, scabies, and chicken pox continue to multiply.

Fortunately, for hospitals that were ready to collapse, the first shipments of medicine arrive. The drugs are so badly needed that they don't even make it to the hospital pharmacies; they are brought straight to the operating rooms and used immediately. The official numbers dispensed by the World Health Organization make the situation clear: in three weeks, forty-six out of the seventy-two clinics in Gaza and twelve of its thirty-five hospitals have closed their doors. They are unable to continue their work because they lack the means to run the generators that supply the necessary electricity; meanwhile, the emergency grows ever greater.

## *The Children's War*

IN KHAN YUNIS A CROWDED café is bombed: twelve people die, including a woman with a Dutch passport. Just a short while before, she had been waiting at the Rafah crossing, hoping to leave. Bombs also fall on Rafah and Deir al-Balah. The excessive number of wounded exhausts the capacities of the ERs. Doctors are forced to operate on patients lying on the ground; they beg everyone to donate blood, which is running out. The morgue is overcrowded too: corpses, wrapped in white sheets, are lined up on the sidewalks near the entrance, and family members are asked to take them away as quickly as possible. But without fuel for their cars, they have no means to do so. And so, for funerals, donkey carts are used instead. At the morgue, the dead bodies of children arrive, their names written with markers on their calves or arms. This is done by their parents, to identify them and keep them from being buried with a number on the bedsheet. "Are these children the enemy?" I hear someone yell.

Forty percent of the victims of bombing in Gaza are minors. This statistic comes from UNICEF, not the Gaza Ministry of Health. And things are no better for the youth who survive. You see them senseless from fear, in shock from the loss of their families, the devastation of the only world they'd ever known. There are more orphans than can be counted. Hearing them call out the names of dead mothers, fathers, sisters, and brothers, your heart breaks. They cry in desperation, begging to be brought to homes that no longer exist. Meanwhile, the eldest among them speak of death as if it were normal, in reference to themselves, "If I don't die, I would like ..."

I go each day to Al-Aqsa Hospital in Deir al-Balah to recharge my phone, because they have electricity from their solar panels. I meet colleagues there to exchange information, and I also become friends with Salma. She is ten years old and has been left alone to care for her little brothers, aged two and five. Her mother and an elder sister are there too, being treated; they are in grave condition, but the rest of her family has been killed by bombs. These three small survivors sleep outside with other children, alone like them. It's hard to help them get over their terror; it makes them wet the bed and leaves them listless, with no appetite. The NGOs that should take care of them are in chaos. Teenagers have volunteered to look after them: athletic youngsters organize them in improvised team competitions; young girls recite fairy tales or lead them in song. Others manage to transform clothesline into jump ropes, build small villages from cardboard boxes, or use scrap paper for drawing. It's touching to see how tightly the children grip every toy they play with, knowing it may be ripped from them tomorrow.

In the shelters, mothers try to maintain a minimum of order, wiping their faces, hands, and teeth with barely moistened rags. They try to give the children a few school lessons as well, tracing letters from the alphabet on the ground or on the walls of what once were classrooms. "My children are sleeping in the cold, in filth," complains a widow named Jannat, as her three young boys roll around on mattresses in a tent pitched near the hospital. "What human rights do my sons have?"

Elsewhere, in Rafah, I meet Yazan. He is thirteen and from Shuja'iyya. He and his sister Jasmine, who is eleven, are the only two survivors of the air strike that destroyed their home. They first saw their mother's body unearthed from the rubble, then their father's, their sisters' and brothers'—all dead. He is in shock, obviously traumatized by what has happened to him, but he is also up front about it. He speaks of the tragedy to everyone, summing it up simply, "We were six kids. Now four of us are dead, and two are alive. I'm the man of the family now; I have to take care of my sister." He feels

*Yazan Harazin, from the Shuja'iyya neighborhood in eastern Gaza City.*

responsible for the little girl—all that's left of his family. I look at him in admiration, asking myself how a child his age can be so resilient, after the shock of a bombing and seeing the bodies of his loved ones recovered. He tells me that he went by himself to the hospital. He got his wounds cleaned and then went back to search for his family. "My mother and father were found quickly. It took a whole day to find my siblings." He respects journalists. "I want to have your job." Why? "You listen—even to me, and I'm only a boy. I want to tell the stories of people like you do." He touches the fabric of my flak jacket. "It's too heavy for a child," I say. He looks me in the eye. "I can do it," he says. So I help him into it and snap a photo of him looking proud, weighed down with the pain of a land that turns boys into old men. One day I hope to give it to him.

These children see their world collapsing around them. They read the terror in their parents' faces. There are bombings and tank assaults that go on for over thirty minutes. The attacks blow out your eardrums, turning your mind to mush. In such moments the youngest scream in desperation. All you can do is hug them tight. It isn't easy. You can't hide your own fear; they know you're lying if you try to reassure them. The only way to calm them—later, after the worst has passed, and the eldest have gotten ahold of themselves—is to play with them. Trying to get them to forget that last hour.

To do this, I've found a secret weapon: a Rubik's Cube. A boy who is staying with us brought it. I already knew the trick for solving it, and now I brandish it whenever the bombs fall, as if it were magic. I egg them on, "Keep going, keep going," whenever they flinch. And it works. They get hypnotized.

## *Profession: Reporter*

THE HEAD OF THE AL Jazeera news office for the Strip, Wael Al-Dahdouh—who goes by al Jabal ("the mountain")—is reporting live as always on October 25, describing the nonstop attacks on Gaza, when someone comes up and whispers in his ear. The building in Nuseirat where his family has found shelter has been hit by the bombing. He runs off. The TV cameras follow him as he hurries away, first home and then to the hospital, where he holds the dead body of his barely seven-year-old daughter, Sham, in his arms. "They're revenging themselves by killing children," he cries. "This attack was targeted." We then see him at the Deir al-Balah morgue, bidding goodbye to his wife, Amna, his nephew, Adam, and eight other relatives. Bent over his fifteen-year-old son, Mahmoud, he gives one last caress: "He wanted to be a journalist." When he leaves the hospital, he begins to report live again. I have no idea how he finds such courage.

I know him well; we spend a lot of time together. He's from an important family and is a veteran reporter from Gaza. He has worked with Al Jazeera since 2004. Before that, he wrote for the newspaper *Al-Quds* and worked for Al Arabiya TV as well. In 2013, he was given the Next Century Foundation's Peace through Media Award.

His personal tragedy, lived out in front the same TV cameras that had been filming him reporting live, is caught by footage seen instantly across the world, turning him into a reluctant symbol of the difficulty of reporting from Gaza. In the weeks to come, the Israelis will make him pay dearly. And sure enough, on December 15, while covering the air strike on the Haifa School in Khan Yunis, he and a cameraman Samer Abu Daqqa are hit by a missile; his colleague bleeds out, and he is wounded as well. He returns to work, his arm in a sling under his bulletproof PRESS jacket. Next, on January 7, his eldest son, Hamza Al-Dahdouh, a cameraman for Al Jazeera, is killed. Twenty-seven years old. Two other nephews die in an air strike the next day. At that point, on January 16, after 102 days of war and tireless work in the field, with help from TV Qatar, he leaves. The Egyptian authorities allow him to cross at Rafah; he is brought to Doha, where he recovers and where, so far as I know, he still resides.

*Sami (center) with his fellow reporters.*
*On the far left, his close friend Sami Abu Salem.*

In the meantime, another journalist friend of mine is killed, Mohammad Abu Hattab. When our colleague, Salman Al Bashir finds this out while reporting live, he takes off his helmet and flak jacket. "Kill me too," he says. "After all, it's just a question of time."

Before the war there were 640 "official" journalists: reporters who had obtained a press card from the Palestinian Journalists Syndicate. We stay in contact by using the chat rooms of various government ministers. Some of these write for the independent or foreign newspapers—Arab, American, Chinese, Russian—that are not allowed to have their own reporters in the field. Only a few work with the Europeans and communicate with them, as I do, in English. Others work freelance; lacking any concrete job prospects, they invent a career for themselves by doing photojournalism or livestream commentaries. This phenomenon—citizen journalism—has grown spontaneously since the beginning of the conflict. With the help of cell phones, young men and women tell the war stories they see outside their windows and in their everyday lives. Then they publish their pictures on social media. They're really talented; I follow many of them.

It was dangerous already to be a journalist in Gaza; neither Hamas nor Israel ever valued our work. Since the war began, it's much worse. Not only because Israel has blocked 3G networks, making it more difficult to find internet connections and file our stories. Also because in the stories we tell we're not simply observers, we're also protagonists. We may die. Or find out that we have friends or relatives among the victims of a tragedy we're covering. This happened to yet another of my colleagues, again, while reporting live. He was broadcasting from a hospital, and he came across the dead bodies of his sister and her children. It broke him—he could no longer speak.

We leave home not knowing if we'll return, or if we'll come back and find our home still standing. For wives and children, it's torture too. They know we go to dangerous places where a blue bulletproof vest isn't enough to protect us. It will get worse. Before long, "reporter" will become another word for target.

## *Bisan's Wounds*

**Al Dahdouh's tragedy brings me** back to the day when my daughter Bisan was severely wounded by Israeli shrapnel and lost three fingers on one hand. It was November in 2012, she was eight years old, and, just like my colleague, I was working. The day before Ahmed al-Jabari, the leader of the Ezzedin Al-Qassam Brigade, had been killed along with his son, in a targeted strike by Israel. A missile had hit his car as it drove down a street in Gaza. Hamas reacted by firing off rockets, and Israel responded with Operation Pillar of Defense, destroying an arsenal of Fajr-3 missiles in Gaza. I was covering the Jabari funeral when I got the news: Bisan had been wounded in the courtyard of our home by a stray piece of shrapnel. She was in Al-Shifa Hospital, where they were trying to save her hand. I rushed there.

Over the years, she has had to undergo many operations, and, from that day on, she has suffered from trauma, as has her twin sister, Ruba, who was there at the time. During the bombings, they hug each other tightly; it's endearing but devastating to watch. They want me to stay with them, telling me they only feel safe when I'm there. As a result, I've had to work less. It hasn't always been easy to both work and rush to their side. Before they were adults, we didn't live together, which made it even harder.

I married their mother, Suad, in 2001. We were both thirty-four years old. It was a traditional marriage—in other words, arranged. The twins were born in 2004. Ours wasn't a perfect marriage, and, after a few years, we decided to split up—a difficult decision in such a restrictive society. The girls grew up with her. By law, they have to stay with the mother until they are twelve, after that, the father decides. They were already coming to my place twice a week; then, when they turned eighteen, they moved in with me. It was their choice; they had more freedom with me than they did with their mother. For some time already, out of love for the two of them, relations between Suad and me had improved. And she's actually been relieved that the girls have been with me since the war began. She trusts my choices. In the most difficult months, she was in Khan Yunis, at the Red Crescent headquarters, surrounded by tanks for weeks, without food or other resources. For ten days, we had no news from her, and the girls were very afraid. Fortunately, she was safe. Since then, Ruba and Bisan phone her constantly, many times a day.

## *Ground Offensive*

**Israel has found a new** way to make us suffer: the imposition of a communications blackout from Friday, October 27, through dawn on Sunday, October 29, with the lines opened briefly at 4:00 AM, then down again. We're cut off from the world, with no news from our loved ones and no information about what is happening around us. With no means to communicate, we journalists can't work at all. We all gather at the hospital in Deir al-Balah, where there is electricity, so we can charge our phones. Even people with satellite phones don't have any connection. The only news we get comes visually, from the distant smoke of bombs or the arrival of more dead and wounded—many of them children—carried in or brought on whatever cart or wagon happens to be at hand. Unfortunately, with no communication, it isn't possible to know where ambulances are needed.

Both north and south of the Strip, the population lives through forty-eight endless hours of terror and anguish. These sensations are heightened by two consecutive nights of constant noise of bombing and sirens that let no one sleep. The torment of not hearing from their loved ones also keeps them awake. These fears, in some cases, are well-founded. When communication is restored at last, it results in a flood of grief and bad news. Above all, we learn that the ground offensive has begun.

North of Wadi Gaza, there is rubble everywhere. Blockaded roads, corpses, and another river of people fleeing south unable to carry anything with them. Only two hospitals are left standing: in Rimal, Al-Shifa is under siege. According to Israel, there are militants either inside or in subterranean tunnels, yet the hospital is packed with refugees and the wounded—if it were bombed, there would be a bloodbath.

The doctors in Al-Quds Hospital are again told they must evacuate, despite the fact that 25,000 people are inside. It has become a sort of village: in an entrance that looks like a lunar landscape from bombs that fell fifty yards away, there is even a market, packed with carts. The World Health Organization repeats, "It is impossible to evacuate without risking the lives of patients."

The Strip has now been cut in two, that much is certain. And a raid on October 31 terrorizes us further: six bombs, each weighing a ton, destroy an entire city block in Jabalia—one of the most densely populated places on earth, where 30 percent of the residents have not evacuated. More than fifty die, most of them children. At least four hundred are wounded. They get transported by any means available to the so-called Indonesian Hospital, named after the country that funded its construction. Headquartered in Beit Lahia, it has only one hundred beds; for weeks already, the number of patients there has been ten times its capacity.

Various videos of the massacre circulate. You hear laments and calls for help and see dozens of men trying to dig with their bare hands. You see survivors looking for their loved ones, witnesses to this butchery of bodies. In another film, you see the crowd rejoice when one baby is pulled out of the rubble unharmed, followed quickly by a second. But the bombs have fallen on a densely populated area; under the rubble, there are surely many more dead. Twenty-five apartment complexes have been razed to the ground with a military tactic called "Ring of Fire"—a concise type of raid where bombs are dropped simultaneously along an entire row of buildings, each facing the main street. The Israeli Army announces that the raid killed Ibrahim Biari, commander of the Jabalia Battalion, and destroyed the command post in the area.

The house of my uncle is also flattened, but he escapes. He tells me about the heartrending cries he heard coming from under a collapsed apartment building. They screamed all through the night, and the next morning they were still screaming, until their voices became fainter and fainter. Torture for those trying to free those poor souls, digging with whatever tools they could find or their bare hands, yet unable to reach them due to the heavy blocks of fallen cement—with the only crane in the area damaged in the raid. In different conditions, many of those who survived the bombs could have been saved. Instead, they are left to die a slow, horrible death.

Meanwhile there are violent clashes in the North between militants and the army. Hospitals are filled beyond belief. Everyone seeks refuge inside them, because bombs fall very close by. Israeli tanks advance along the Salah-al-Din Road, which runs through the whole territory up to the edge of the Zeitoun and Shuja'iyya neighborhoods in Gaza City, and enter just under the Wadi, chosen by them as the demarcation line. They shoot at anything that moves. Yet another raid strikes Nuseirat, to the point where people are forced to reopen old tombs and stuff them with bodies, piling new and old corpses together. If it continues like this, the cemeteries won't be able to hold all the dead.

Panic immediately poisons any residue of reciprocal solidarity: fights break out in the overcrowded shelters, and in many villages the bakeries are taken by assault. Even the UNRWA warehouses are sacked by hundreds of the hungry; they strip them of flour, water, and canned goods. Only when communication is restored do things improve: local police are posted in front of bakeries, and distribution resumes under stricter control. There are arrests, and some of the flour is recovered. Lines form again, longer and more tense because rations get cut in half again to serve as many people as possible. If yesterday we were bringing home fifty loaves a day, now we would have to be happy with twenty-five.

# NOVEMBER

## *Double Passport*

**At last, some good news:** the Rafah crossing is opening for foreigners trapped inside the Strip, for Palestinians with double passports, and for the most severely wounded. A total of 7,000 people will be allowed to exit in groups of 500 each. It will take two weeks to get them all out. For everyone left behind, it's traumatic. Those people had governments fighting on their behalf; now that they're gone, will anyone still worry about us? But it's also a relief—fewer hungry mouths to feed. We're also hoping it's the first step to a ceasefire; people are working on it. The open crossing allows in the first upper-level UN official since the war began, Philippe Lazzarini, the Commissioner-General of UNRWA. He will leave in shock, saying, "In Gaza, I've never seen anything like this."

My car has no gas, so I go to Rafah in a taxi. It's really expensive, but I share the cost with two reporter colleagues. At the crossing, I find the same chaos I'm used to. Some are laughing, relieved that their names are on the list. Some are in despair, despite being on the list, because they're forced to leave family and friends behind. Lama is one of them. Thirty years old, she was born in Sofia to a Palestinian mother and Bulgarian father. She alone in her family has dual citizenship and is therefore authorized to leave. She will leave her mother, Nadia, her husband, and two children behind in Gaza. This difficult decision comes after long debates, and everyone agrees that "someone has to survive." And then there's Read, twenty-four years old with an Austrian passport. He looks back, in tears. "I'll never visit this cemetery again." Also Susan, an "American" because she was born in Dearborn, the most Arab city in the entire US. She works for an NGO and feels "guilty and confused, because she wants to leave."

Those who don't find their names on the list are disappointed and afraid. Like Shared, who posts a video to let off steam. "And there still isn't a single Brazilian on the list of foreign citizens. If they don't kill us by bombs, we'll starve before they let us leave." The fifty thousand residents of Gaza with dual Egyptian and Palestinian citizenship, however, are not allowed to leave the Strip. A flurry of phone calls to the West Bank government officials in Ramallah follow. But, as Fatma, a lawyer friend of mine who herself has an Egyptian passport, tells me, the bureaucrats simply repeat that, for now, there's nothing they can do. "We will consider the requests carefully at the first possible opportunity," they say. But when will that be?

There are also others who, though not foreign citizens, live legally abroad, where they study, work, and pay taxes. For example, Fadi, his wife and three kids, have valid Canadian visas on their passports. And he too sends a storm of phone calls to the embassy, getting only polite reassurances in response. "Every night I look at the list, and each time it's another bitter disappointment."

I meet Amal, a fifty-year-old German Palestinian. After countless struggles with rigid bureaucrats and innumerable second thoughts, she has given up on leaving, because she doesn't want to leave her husband, two grown sons, and their wives, along with her newborn grandchildren. "What sort of life can I live, if everyone I love is in danger of dying?" She is afraid, but still she has decided to share with them this time of hunger and bombs that fall everywhere at any time. The very moment the Rafah crossing opens, a group of refugees is mowed down on Al Rashid Street. "There are corpses of both men and women all along the side of the road," according to witnesses.

In the meantime, the army's vise-grip around Gaza City has grown progressively tighter. Bombings and attacks come from three distinct trajectories. Tel al-Hawa is the site of the Islamic University, the Ministry of the Interior, and residential high-rises, ten-floor apartment buildings built in the 90s, the home of Gaza City's middle-class. Hassan Ashur, a thirty-six-year-old man, lives in one of these buildings, directly in front of Al-Quds Hospital, with his wife and two kids, ages seven and four. They managed to move to the South and tried to live there, only to return to the North, having found the overpopulation in the South truly oppressive. "They would never bomb the neighborhood of the hospital," everyone thought. "Forty thousand people live there." And it was true; for a while, proximity to Al-Quds Hospital did have advantages: medical care at arm's reach, functioning electricity to recharge your phones. Plus, it's a place where aid arrives, so you can find something to eat. At the start of November, however, everything changes quickly.

My friend Hassan calls me in terror. There are soldiers close to his home, and their building is being targeted by artillery. They're hiding in a basement apartment with other families. They're out of food but can't risk going outside. No use trying to get to Al-Quds—there are snipers. And it's no longer safe at the hospital: people have been killed right at the main entrance, and even ambulances full of wounded en route to Egypt have been targeted, despite the fact that the transfers were approved by the army.

Huddled in that cold basement, around a small gas stove barely big enough to boil water for the children, the Ashur family stays in touch with the world by cell phone. They only turn it on from time to time, to save the battery. In one of their many desperate texts, they write, "Is the battle still going on?" I don't have any good news to share. Only some advice: "Ration your food and stay strong."

Meanwhile the Israeli tanks enter from the other side of the city. They destroy the Catholic Sisters of Rosario School as well as Al-Fakhura School, run by UNRWA, both in the Tel al-Hawa neighborhood, near Al-Quds Hospital; fifteen people die. Bombs also fall on the Sheikh Zayed mosque, which, luckily, is empty. In the Al-Maghazi refugee camp, an apartment building is hit. I see the images of survivors intent on digging through the rubble as well as a line of white body bags. They fill forty-seven. A skyscraper is ripped open, and the army offers the usual justification: a Hamas member lived there. But in that same building there was also a photojournalist, Mohammed Alaloul. In the bombing, his four children and three siblings die.

In the Sheikh Radwan neighborhood, a missile strikes the roof of a house. It's the home of my sister Samya. Having been warned by the army, they try to flee by taxi. But the vehicle is unable to reach them. The bombing kills the wife of her oldest son and wounds a granddaughter. Her husband—loath to accept the changes—chose not to move his wife and children to the South. I offer them my apartment in Jabalia. They'll be safe, and they'll also be able to keep an eye on my things, since by now there are thieves everywhere.

## A Month of War

IN JUST THE FIRST WEEK of November, six thousand bombs are dropped. The list of the dead passes ten thousand. Every family is in mourning. No location is safe; Israel is bombing everywhere. Official statements say they are only striking where there are militants, but it isn't true. By this point, Gaza no longer exists. They've already destroyed much of it—including places where there were certainly no militants. A month of war has erased the world I knew.

Each day I think must be the worst. Then the next is still worse. Yet some are more brutal than others—when death comes into your home. On November 6, two of my cousins die along with their families when their homes are bombed. My daughters sob for hours. I'd already seen them crying when they got news that friends had died. But this time they're really desperate. They'd grown up with those cousins. I find no words to comfort them.

The situation is growing more difficult by the day. Each might be the last, but we still scuttle about like ants, gathering what we need to survive one more day.

In the markets you only find cucumbers and peppers, along with rice and lentils. The aid that arrives isn't enough, and the blockade on fuel at the border continues, despite the fact that hospitals can't function without it. And bulldozers too, which are needed to dig the wounded out from beneath the rubble, so instead they die a slow, agonizing death. Even water purification systems are kept out, so we're forced to drink it still contaminated, and infectious diseases have already begun to spread. Gasoline can only be bought on the black market, sold at exorbitant prices by schemers with secret stashes. Some people are running their cars with cooking oil in the gas tank. It stinks to high heaven; the nauseating smell sickens the streets. Everyone is obsessed with water; we dream of it, fresh and clean. We talk about nothing else.

## *Khan Yunis*

**In my sister's by now** overcrowded "chalet" in Deir al-Balah, where I'm living, it's impossible to get an internet connection, and I need to be online to work more easily. I decide to leave my parents there, with my brother Ahmed to take care of them, not to mention my other sister, Siham, who has moved in as well. My daughters and I move to Khan Yunis, to the house of my friend, Saeed al-Agha.

Saeed is an accountant. He's thirty-eight years old and never married; like me, he sees marriage as a prison. We've known each other for years and used to get together every Thursday night—the beginning of our weekend—at our favorite café, Al-Baqa, a famous place on the seaside in Gaza, with a splendid view. Given its reputation as an "underground" club, it's a favorite of all the Strip's rebels and frequented by the most interesting people around: activists, writers, intellectuals, and university students with their professors. Also by women on their own, not wearing the veil, since here, without being bothered, they could smoke a shisha—a hookah with perfumed tobacco. Police raids, though, were a daily affair. They'd come, arrest everyone, and close the place down. And every time, the owner would reopen again. Once they even flattened it with bulldozers, and the owner rebuilt it from scratch. Running that place, he would say, was his mission in life. I brought all the foreign journalists I worked with there, because at that place no one was afraid to talk, everyone was friendly and polite—something that in an insular society like ours can't be taken for granted.

*Close friends. (From the left) Fadi Ali, Fatma Ashour, Saeed al-Agha.*

At Saeed's place, we reconnect with our circle of friends. As it happens, along with us he is hosting my lawyer friend Fatma and her sister. Also a divorced businessman named Mohammed Abbu Shaaban, the manager of an import-export company. His family is there as well: his mother Maysara, a really energetic sixty-year-old who does her best to make us feel at home. She's enthused about cooking for all of us, even though we now total twenty-six. His father, Jaqube, is sick and needs a good deal of care. And his sister with her children, including Sara and Judi, who are just a bit younger than my girls. They become fast friends immediately, spending their days watching TV shows on Bisan's computer and whispering girl talk.

We make a pact with Saeed not to speak too much about the war in front of his folks. In order not to worry them, we spend our time making jokes about the situation we're in. For example, we sing praises for the propane tank we bought for 1,000 shekels (about 260 dollars), twenty times its usual cost. "Give it tender loving care—it has a degree from the Sorbonne." And more silliness of that sort. The al-Agha family is from Khan Yunis, so they know everyone, and they know where you can find the essentials: rice and water. Nonetheless, we are all hungry, so we impose rules on ourselves. Even though we're a community of choice, living together isn't easy. Saeed, Mohammed, and I quickly take on leadership roles. We become something of a triumvirate; we decide how to ration the water and provisions. And cause more than a little unrest as a result.

In the house's courtyard, we jerry-rig a stove that doesn't need propane. Mohammed is the official keeper of the fire. He starts it each morning with cardboard and small branches that we gather from outside. We even build our own firepit: three stones and a piece of metal that shelters our fire from the wind. It's my job to make the morning tea for everyone—a very meager breakfast, but at least it warms us up.

We figure out how to find places for everyone to sleep in this two-story house. The women sleep upstairs in beds or mattresses on the floor, which are rolled up every morning. We men sleep downstairs, some on couches, others on improvised bedding. I smoke and snore incessantly, as my daughters never hesitate to point out, so I find myself a spot outside, under the porch. At least there I don't bother anyone. And that's how I get wounded. One night, a bomb falls close by, and all the windows of the house are shattered. Shards of glass hit me in the thigh. At that moment, though, I don't do anything about it; I'm too afraid for the girls. I run upstairs, and I can hardly breathe. Bisan was sleeping right under a window, and now she's covered by thick curtains strewn with glass. Luckily, the curtains protected her. We spend an hour taking off the shards of glass, while she lies there motionless, frozen with fear.

There's one more reason why living with friends is such a blessing. So many other families, just normal people like us, have suddenly found themselves in places stuffed with strangers, with no privacy, and having to put up with forced intimacy between men and women can be even worse than the hunger, given that most of them are culturally conservative. In the initial stages, they tried to maintain divisions—women staying inside and men out in the open. But as it got colder, sleeping separately became impossible.

In overcrowded classrooms and in tent cities, where spaces are divided with "walls" formed by clotheslines, young women and men have started talking with each other. To tell the truth, they'd been doing it already, in secret, with their smartphones. Now they no longer can hide, and this triggers fights and feuds. Shotgun weddings result.

Unfortunately, Palestinians in Gaza are more traditional than those in the West Bank when it comes to religious restrictions, which prohibit any form of promiscuity. For years now, we've all been living one life in the open and another in secret, or as we say, "hidden under the table"—our term for everything not socially acceptable and hence disguised.

## *A Hospital Under Siege*

The bombs that collapsed the building in front of Al-Quds Hospital also blocked access to the facility. Snipers are shooting at anything that moves, preventing the removal of rubble. Patients, doctors, and 40,000 refugees are trapped inside the structure. This news comes from an eyewitness: my brother Hassan, who manages the facility and is there inside. Even the top two floors of the hospital were hit; there are two dead and various other casualties. The situation is dire; a passageway must be opened ASAP. "With no medicine or electricity, doctors are having to decide who lives and who dies, who gets put on a ventilator, and who gets a lifesaving drug or a leg amputation," Hassan tells me. "Whoever is strongest, whoever has the best chance of survival, gets favored, but the choice is atrocious." These cruel decisions must be made in an instant, working under the worst possible conditions: operating on the floor, with no anesthesia, disinfectants, or even water to wash your hands. In the middle of children crying and the chatter of the crowd that packs every inch of the building. The doctors are saving lives at the cost of their own; already, just in the first month, 160 of them have been killed at work, according to figures given by the World Health Organization.

Before the war, there were 5,600 health-care workers in the entire enclave. Of the doctors, 600 were general practitioners; only 350 had specializations. The rest were nurses, orderlies, and other support staff. Given the emergency situation, medical students have been called in as well. Already there weren't enough doctors for two and half million people, so you can imagine how it is now, with enormous numbers of wounded—more than 25,000. By now, due to the bombing as well as the lack of fuel and medicine, fifteen of the thirty-five hospitals have closed, including the only clinic that treats tumors. "It's a tragedy," says Shawqi Muhaisen, a well-known neurologist in Gaza. "We've been completely abandoned. We're on our own." Even so, while sacrificing themselves beyond any conceivable limit, taking shifts that last for an entire week, sleeping on gurneys because it's too dangerous to go home, they succeed in offering dignified care, taking into consideration the extreme conditions they work under.

Like everyone else, they're dealing with the daily risks their families face. Thirty-four-year-old Mahmud al-Astal was working a shift at the Nasser Hospital ER in Khan Yunis when he found himself in front of his sister and her kids, "in pieces, burned to a crisp." Others have found their own children, their parents, their wives or husbands on the operating table—and yet they couldn't give in to the emotion and pain. They had to stay lucid, no matter what, and for that they are true heroes. Though no one asks them, or thanks them for it, they also take on the burden of caring for orphans; some children arrive at the hospital with gravely injured parents who quickly pass away. The medical staff doesn't abandon these children. They comfort them, feed them, and take care of them until they manage to find a relative willing to take them in. And since that isn't always possible, each hospital by now has its own "volunteer" orphanage.

## *Afoot in the Rubble*

**Eleven people walking, carrying their** miserable possessions through rubble and human remains for over ten hours. How long does it take to cover fifteen rough, dangerous miles on foot? They're trying to get to the south side of the Strip, taking advantage of the umpteenth north-south corridor opened for a couple of hours by Israel. After a long odyssey, on the morning of November 8, the Kahwel family—Father Khaled, Mother Ahisa, and their nine children (the youngest just four, the oldest twenty-two)—manages to reach the so-called safe area below Wadi Gaza.

"The hike here was terrible. We're exhausted, numb, especially the kids," the head of family explains, describing their voyage through hell, which begun at 4:00 AM in Beit Lahia, one of the towns farthest north in the Strip. "The recent attacks forced us to go. The bombing got more and more powerful, capable of convulsing the depths of the earth, because they were targeting the tunnels. They blew up the last supermarket in our area. When my wife told me that if the bombs didn't kill us, we'd die of starvation, since tree bark and leaves were all we had left, I made up my mind." After weeks in hiding, they faced the journey out. "Even in my worst nightmares, I never could have dreamed of what we've found. If I'd known I would be exposing my kids to this sort of torture, I might have had second thoughts." It wasn't just the long line of neighborhoods in ruin that shocked them. "It's impossible to take a direct route. We had to go through the old city and then Zeitoun before getting to Salah al-Din Road." Above all, he told me, "We came across hundreds of unburied corpses. The bodies of men, women, and children were obscene—rendered unrecognizable from fire or the animals, rats, or birds that were feasting on them." The horror was such that they had to blindfold the youngest children and make them walk in a line, with the eldest closing out the rueful procession.

The most terrifying moment, however, happened when they had to walk past an Israeli tank stationed on high ground, controlling the entire crossing from north to south. "We used a shirt as a white flag. We went past with our arms raised as a sign of surrender. Everyone, even the children." When they reached the other side, they were exhausted. Only the last four miles were easy. Family members already in the south arranged for a taxi to bring them to the Al-Maghazi refugee camp—where they would be safe, more or less, since bombs had fallen there as well. "We're still together and everyone's alive. We have food," he said. "I can't know our future, but certain death is a little farther off."

Amid thousands of displaced persons, I meet Noor Hammad. She's twenty-four years old and, until a month ago, she was happy. Working in a clinic as a nutritionist, she was recently married and is expecting her first child. Seven months pregnant, previously she hadn't felt up to traveling the twelve miles on foot to get below Wadi Gaza. But now the risk was too great, so she set off, with her husband, Hassan. And she made it, even if she had to stop many times, when the baby was kicking or the hunger and thirst had become unbearable. In Khan Yunis, they knocked on UNRWA's door, asking for a small corner to stay in, at least for her and her bulging belly. They received vouchers for extra food from UNRWA storehouses, but in the overcrowded building, no one would lend her their spot to bed down. So next they tried at Nasser Hospital. It was packed too; because there was no emergency, they also sent them away. A wearying pilgrimage. Finally, at the home of a friend of his sister, they were welcomed in; they share the space with twenty-five others. They have a roof over their heads, but Noor is sleeping on the floor. The joy of an expectant mother has turned into unending anxiety: "Where will I deliver my baby? Who will help me? How will I keep the child warm? Will I be able to nurse it and keep it alive?

Noor isn't the only one worried about her baby. Data from the Ministry of Health suggests that at least fifty thousand women are currently pregnant in Gaza. In a shared declaration, UNICEF, the UN Population Fund, and the World Health Organization have released additional troubling data. On average, since the beginning of the war, 180 women each day have given birth in the worst possible conditions, some of them "in the streets, amid the rubble." Those who manage to get to a hospital have traumatic deliveries. With no anesthesia and a lack of available drugs, mothers are immediately sent home, no matter how exhausted they are. Some newborns are so sickly and scrawny that they end up in incubators, but the incubators are powered by solar panels, which have, in some cases, been destroyed by bombing. There are no figures on how many babies have died as a result. With the number of wounded, in the hospitals, no one has any time left for postpartum care. "Maternal deaths are expected to increase," the three agencies affirm in their shared statement, as well as the "risks of malnutrition, disease and death.". They also predict "a rise in stress-induced miscarriages, stillbirths and premature births." Noor is praying that the war will end soon.

"The baby will be born in January. And, I hope, in peacetime."

## *In the Line of Fire: Khan Yunis*

LATE IN THE EVENING OF November 15, the Israeli army announces with leaflets dropped from planes that their operations will be extended around Khan Yunis, an area that until now has been designated as safe. The first calls to evacuate are directed to residents on the eastern side of the city, the villages of Al-Qarara, Khuza'a, Bani Suheila, and Abasan. Written in Arabic, the flyers read, "For safety reasons, leave your premises immediately." They state that, "The actions of Hamas force us to operate in your residential districts." The inhabitants of these areas, over sixty thousand people, waste no time; long columns of new refugees begin to move. Carts carry whatever they can pile on them: clothing, bedding, pots and pans, the precious propane tanks, cats, and goats. They fear that anything left behind will be lost forever. The umpteenth internal displacement: this one is particularly discouraging, since these prominently agricultural areas provide some of the vegetables still in the markets. Soon it will be more difficult to find fresh food. In the meantime, the last working gristmill—As Salam in Deir al-Balah—was destroyed by bombs, so flour can no longer be produced locally.

The million and a half people already packed into the southern Strip are an additional problem. There's no more room. "Where should we go?" wails Mohammed al-Haitham, a farmer from Abasan, arriving with his wife and six children. The recommendation is to head for Rafah, the southernmost point of the Strip. Since the Palestinians with double nationality have left, there is space in the schools, at least for now. UNRWA has some tents set up on the beach as well. But it rains, the canvas gets soaked through, and water drenches the bedding and clothing of the unfortunate who shelter there, making their stored food moldy. Nonetheless, the rain does bring some relief. Potable water is precious, and many people manage to fill jerrycans and buckets. Mothers take soap and wash their children as if under a shower. Others wash their sheets and clothes *en plein air*.

Icy wind accompanies the rain—a real gale blows in from the sea, strong enough to sweep away UNRWA's tent city. This is also a problem for those of us who are indoors. With no gas left, we can no longer cook. We've been preparing our meals on fire pits outside. We're forced to improvise makeshift grills inside. They do provide heat, but smoke permeates everything.

The torrential rains swamp the mounds of accumulated garbage. Left without basic maintenance, the sewer system fails. Streams of water mixed with excrement and effluent from the trash in the streets increase the risk of epidemics. Mothers constantly yell at their children, warning them not to touch anything. But how is this possible?

With the first wave of cold weather, everyone in my home falls ill—coughing, sore throats, diarrhea—and we catch viruses from each other. We stretch plastic sheets over windows destroyed by the bombing, but it doesn't keep out the cold. In fact, there's another reason we're coughing: the air is polluted. The bombing has released chemical dust and fine particles of asbestos. The World Health Organization states that such substances will produce severe health consequences for years to come; they predict a future of tumors and leukemia similar to the fate of first-responders after the Twin Towers collapsed. At the moment, though, we're more worried about intestinal problems from the contaminated water and spoiled food. Illnesses that are easy to treat, except when the necessary medicine is gone. Aid that arrives consists mainly of the supplies that hospitals need to treat the wounded: pain medication, disinfectants, and the antibiotics urgently needed in the North, where UNRWA speaks of "horribly wounded children on stretchers, with nothing to end their suffering." But here, over-the-counter medicine is also needed to treat illnesses that, if neglected, could become lethal.

Jaqube, the father of my friend Saeed and the oldest among us, is diabetic and has run out of insulin, which can't be found even on the black market. His wife, Maysara, has a heart condition. In other households, people suffer from tumors or autoimmune diseases. For any of them, our forced isolation could become a death sentence, even without the bombs.

In a situation already at the edge, PalTel, the Palestinian telephone company, runs out of fuel for its generators, and cell phones all across the Strip are silent. For twenty-four hours, all communication is down, and then, during the night between November 17 and 18, Israel decides to allow in a minimal quantity of fuel. The need is absolute to reactivate the telephone network and to power the water and sewage systems. It's the first shipment since the beginning of military operations. The agreement is to allow thirty thousand gallons of gasoline every forty-eight hours. "Half of what is needed each day," says UNRWA. "We will be forced to make difficult choices about which systems to run."

In the South, what little food there is becomes scarcer. We're not yet at the point of starvation, but there are fights at the market to grab the last peppers or a handful of potatoes, for which the price jumps from five to fifteen shekels (from around a buck and quarter to almost four dollars). The price of salt is up from two to twenty shekels. The situation is so desperate that there are even people selling UNRWA food rations—packages with canned meat, tuna, lentils, and beans inside—in exchange for blankets, batteries, or diapers. If you can prove you have small children, you are entitled to received powdered milk—but that you need to mix with water, and there's little of that. Women are slipping spoonfuls into everything they serve, hoping they might enrich the meager meals.

The black market is illegal but it has exploded. Gasoline is the biggest money-maker: eighteen liters (just under five gallons) now sells for 1,000 shekels—over $260. Figuring out how to get by is an everyday task. In front of bakeries are lines that last for hours.

Four shekels now buys fifty rolls, according to the "political" price, propped up, in fact, thanks to the flour supplied by UNRWA. But some people wait in line for others and then sell the bread at inflated prices—twenty shekels. The same thing for cigarettes. The price of a pack has gone from eighteen to thirty-six shekels. I'm a heavy smoker, and I suffer when I can't. I buy myself five single cigarettes a day. People who can't afford that pop tranquilizers instead; the pharmacies have kept their price stable, provided you can find a doctor to prescribe them. But that's not hard.

After all, we all suffer from anxiety.

## *A Graveyard for Children*

In the hell of northern Gaza, one place has become a damnation for the living and the dead: Al-Shifa Hospital, now become a cemetery. Squeezed by the total siege imposed by the Israeli army as they hunt down militants, the hospital can no longer bury its dead. The soldiers shoot at anything that moves, despite the fact that there are 650 patients, thousands of refugees, and 500 doctors inside. They don't even grant permission to take the dead outside to be buried; for this reason, the hospital's director, Mohamed Abu Salmiya, has taken the horrifying decision to dig a mass grave inside the hospital's twelve-acre structure in order to bury the two hundred bodies already in some state of decomposition. Among them are seven premature infants who died in non-functioning incubators. Also twenty-nine patients from intensive care who died when the hospital equipment stopped due to lack of fuel.

The work is devastating; to complete it takes a hundred people seven hours. "We had no other choice," states Salmiya. "With no refrigeration, the stench of cadavers from the morgue had become unbearable, and there was also risk of other infectious diseases." It isn't even possible to remove the bodies of those who've died outside the hospital walls—people in need of treatment had dragged themselves there, only to be left, abandoned. As Mohammed Obeid, a surgeon working for Médecins Sans Frontières, explains, "The Israelis even shot at the ambulances we sent to help those poor souls." Their corpses attract starving stray dogs that feast on the meager remains.

Lured by the smell of death, these animals—that no one shoots—come inside the hospital grounds, putting the patients at added risk. The situation is tragic. UNICEF offers its testimony, calling the North of Gaza, a "graveyard for children." This is not mere rhetoric: 40 percent of the victims are minors. The same wretched system forced upon the hospital also happens at home; they are digging tombs inside their courtyards. Where there is no courtyard, they pull up the flooring in basements or even in apartments, just to offer their loved ones a burial—and to defend themselves from disease.

Elsewhere, a terrible siege lasting over two weeks forces the evacuation of Gaza's other major hospital, Al-Quds. The soldiers have been targeting it since the end of October. My brother Hassan is there, inside. To support him, I go every day to visit his wife and sons in Khan Yunis. The battle rages around the walls of the hospital, and for two weeks it's impossible to enter or exit the building. Only at mid-month does the logjam break. The Red Crescent negotiates for days with the Israeli military authorities, and they finally reach an agreement for evacuating the structure on November 12. The operation is complex, given that the medical center has no electricity; by now it is without water and food, so treating patients has become impossible.

And so, a procession of trucks and ambulances loaded with patients manages to reach Wadi Gaza, but then, after having searched them from top to bottom, the soldiers send them back. Too much fighting in the area, they say. A second evacuation order arrives early in the afternoon of November 14—not via official channels. The army calls my brother Hassan directly on his cell phone, warning him, "You have twenty minutes to evacuate." The chaos is unimaginable. But they do manage to squeeze dozens of people into whatever vehicles they find—those who are strong enough go on foot. It takes many hours to get through a stretch of road that in normal times you'd cover by car in twenty minutes. The convoy is guided by the army via radio, but they keep finding roads blocked by rubble, forcing them to wait for instructions while vehicles with their tragic human cargo overheat in the sun. During this process, three people die, including a three-year-old girl. Before letting the procession of ambulances pass, everyone must be identified. Even the gravely ill and the medical equipment get inspected. Hassan cries at length as he tells me about it.

Below the Wadi Gaza line, hospitals are also in desperate straits. And it's difficult to treat children sick with cancer or leukemia: the oldest is fourteen, the youngest barely a year old. Thanks to the White House's direct intervention, they are given permission to leave the Strip and go to Egypt or Jordan. Twenty-one of them get out, but thirty others remain trapped in labyrinthian channels of communication and bureaucracy. Some families get the messages summoning them to the border too late, and they miss their window. Others wait for days in vain for the ambulances. The parents of a small boy, at the Rafah crossing, discover that they haven't been put on the list of accompanying family members; they are forced to make the agonizing decision whether to send their son on alone, not knowing if they'll ever see him again.

Finally, on November 19, a convoy of seven ambulances sent by the World Health Organization enters through the Rafah crossing with the special mission of taking to safety the thirty-one preemies trapped at Al-Shifa, where the battle was concentrated. A photo that went viral showed these same newborns grouped together in a single crib, so that they would keep each other warm after the incubators stopped due to the lack of electricity. In the meantime, two die. By the final week, a total of twelve don't manage to survive. The others—born too soon and at the worst possible moment—leave the hospital with three doctors and two nurses, but without their mothers, who aren't allowed to leave.

# A Fragile Truce

**Our days move to the** beat of echoes from news bulletins, which play on thousands of transistor radios everywhere. We listen to the Palestinian broadcasts from Ramallah: Sawt El Ghad, Radio Angham, Turath Radio. There's a strong signal, and they also feature extensive excerpts from Al-Jazeera TV news shows. In contrast, the Gaza stations, including Al-Aqsa, have been silent for more than a month. We're stressed out, waiting. After days of bombing, rain, and bad news, we're hoping for only one headline: an agreement for a prisoner exchange and temporary ceasefire. To us, after six weeks of horror, the prospect of a few days of peace seems the best that could happen. We hope for so many things, and our greatest wish is to once again hug our family members stuck in the North. Of course, some of us are hoping for small things too, like sleeping without terror from the bombs for an entire night. Or to get hold of better food, tents, blankets, maybe even less makeshift lodging. Out of many urgent needs, one is moving the dead we've buried nearby, a potential source of disease. Negotiations simply can't fail.

With that in mind, we begin to speak again about the future: returning home, rebuilding. And about politics: a new government without Hamas. There are two major theories. First is an executive branch led by Mohammed Dahlan, the former leader of the Fatah party here in Gaza. He lives in Abu Dhabi, where he has been very successful, but he's from Khan Yunis and has strong local ties. An enemy of Hamas, he is also an opponent of the Palestinian Authority head, Abu Mazen, whom he accuses of conspiring to depose him. He could work to form a civil government while the UN or Israelis manage security operations for a time. The other theory is the return of the Palestinian Authority; as old as Abu Mazen is now, though, it's hard to see who would be chosen to lead. What is certain is that the government of Gaza is in ruins politically; its militants and officials are no longer seen in the streets. That doesn't mean as a movement it's finished—difficult for it to completely disappear. For now, anyway, most Gazans no longer want to hear talk about them.

Hope, desperation, hope anew. Only after days of roller-coasting does the headline happen: together with the exchange of fifty Israeli hostages for 150 Palestinian prisoners, a four-day ceasefire has been agreed on, beginning on the morning of November 24. It had been scheduled to start on the 22nd; when the news of this deferral arrives, late the day before, it causes many to panic about new military initiatives—and new victims. And, in fact, bombings do follow, east of Khan Yunis, on the outskirts of Deir al-Balah and on Nuseirat. One hundred and sixty die, including fifty members of a single family, the Qadoura. Everyone is killed, from grandparents to grandchildren. A method of pressuring the militants to accept the final details of this strict agreement.

Confirmation arrives at last. The agreement allows for roughly 200 trucks to enter Gaza, loaded with aid. And more fuel: four tankers per day—not enough, though, to start up again everything that has been halted for a month and a half. The first day we celebrate, euphoric after a night with no bombs. When the truce goes into effect at 7:00 AM, the streets rapidly fill up, with some folks leaving their homes for the first time. The elderly set their chairs out in the pallid autumn sun; children dive into games uninhibited. Family members and friends meet up again. I see people hugging everywhere. The most crowded place is the market; even if there isn't much to sell, at last goods can be bought without fear of dying under the bombs.

In the North, the situation is different. Roadblocks are everywhere; movement remains constrained. Only Salah al-Din Road is accessible, and only in one direction, going south. Dropping leaflets at dawn, the army reaffirms, "The war isn't over. The pause is temporary. For your security, remain in the South. The North is a military zone." To little effect. The joy of the truce fools many.

Groups of men head north any way they can: on foot, with bicycles, on donkey carts. There are cars as well—only a few, but filled to overflowing, with people hanging onto hoods and roofs. "We want to bury our dead, recover remains from under the rubble, help the parents we left behind. We want to see our houses again and get our clothes, our blankets, our pots and pans." Things go badly. When they get up to Wadi Gaza, scuffles break out; the Israelis start shooting and kill two people, wounding seven. Nothing to do except turn around.

New aid trucks arrive, honking their horns. There ought to be 200, but by nightfall there are just 137. UNRWA protests; the Israeli inspections are going too slowly. Thirty thousand tons of provisions, over thirty thousand gallons of gasoline, and three trucks loaded with propane canisters cross into Gaza. For the first time, it's legally possible to bring aid to the North, where a half million people are living in desperate conditions.

On the morning of the 24th, journalists reach the Rafah crossing, expecting the release of Israeli prisoners, a crucial part of the agreement. But the first group of thirteen are instead given over in secret to the Red Crescent in front of the Nasser Hospital in Khan Yunis; they are then transferred using a secondary gate that usually serves only for the transport of merchandise. We don't see them cross. Instead, for an instant, the van carrying Philippine and Thai workers who had been kidnapped along with the Israelis, darts past us.

On their cell phones, people see celebrations in the West Bank, where they are singing and dancing in front of the bus with the first Palestinian prisoners freed from Israeli prisons, exchanged for hostages as part of the accord. "They celebrate while we're here, getting bombed for weeks," a woman declares, heatedly. "It's disrespectful."

"A four-day truce—barely enough to get a full tank of gas" is the bitter joke on everyone's lips. Unfortunately, it's true. After weeks without fuel, the arrival of tanker trucks allows gas stations in the South to reopen. Still, to fill up your tank, you need to face a line that lasts not for hours, but for days. At least two, nights included; in order not to lose our place, we take turns. To take possession of a three-gallon propane canister, the wait is somewhat less: just a day and a half.

The police take care of maintaining order in the miles-long lines. The officers have suddenly changed their usual behavior: they've taken off their uniforms, and they're more polite. They do everything they can to provide information and work to make sure the distribution of aid is successful. They maintain a careful distance from the higher-ups, just in case there's a change of administration. "I'm a father, and I have a family. I've never been political," says Ahmed, a fifty-year-old sergeant. Even the damaged phone lines get repaired, making it easier to communicate with the North. I hadn't heard anything from my sister Samya, and I was fearing the worst for her and for my home. Instead, she's fine, and the building is still standing.

The truce is incredibly fragile. In the north, there are violations of the ceasefire on both sides.

## *The Power of Women*

**The true heroes in this** war are women. I see them suffer in silence, their husbands prone to violence, and their children increasingly malnourished.

In a refugee camp in western Khan Yunis, I meet forty-five-year-old Yafa, who has a husband and eight kids. Fed up with not having any water, she cut her hair super-short with kitchen scissors, by herself, while everyone was sleeping. When her husband finds out, he's furious; around here, long hair is equated with beauty. Even so, other women followed her example. And they all now have short hair under their veils. In the camp, where water is rationed, it's a necessity. With one turn at a shower every fifteen days, it's not possible to keep hair long.

"Islamic law in Gaza puts us women under the absolute protection of the men in the family," she explains. "This means that conservative men like my husband dispose of us as they please. Now they're less violent than usual, though, because they see how our contribution to the family is crucial."

Each day requires an immense amount of housework. Yafa continually straightens up the tent because, with this mess of people in such a small space, you can never find anything. She lights a fire for cooking. Since she's used to modern appliances, it isn't easy for her to find wood and keep the flames going until nightfall. And she also takes care of the children. She doesn't let them go out. "If they got dirty, I wouldn't know how to wash them." To clean them off from time to time, she marches them off to the seaside, over a mile away. She brings along a bottle of water that has already been used for cooking. She lathers them up with sea water, and then, only at the end, does she use her fresh, "recycled" water to get the salt off their skin.

The 838,100 women and girls evacuated from the homes (the data source is UN Women, the lead United Nations agency working on gender equality) also have other, more dramatic and intimate ordeals. A friend confides in me that she's on the pill, so that her menstrual cycle will be slowed. "I take norethisterone tablets, which are usually prescribed for endometriosis. Without water or hygiene products like pads or tampons, we're forced to risk our health this way, since the regular menstrual cycle is also a problem."

# DECEMBER

## *The Ruins of Gaza City*

**Gaza City no longer exists.** Yahya al-Sarraj, the city's mayor, confirms this in an Al Jazeera broadcast replayed on all the Palestinian radio stations on December 1, 2023. The damage is tremendous: "Sixty percent of everything is in ruins. Fifty-five thousand residential buildings have been destroyed, and the city's infrastructure is unusable. Making your way through the ruins is disorienting; points of reference no longer exist, and it's easy to get lost. Thousands of families have lost everything." Neighborhoods like Sheikh Radwan are deserted; the houses have been broken into and looted—by whom, it's difficult to say.

Jabalia is the place where the largest number of people remain. One of these is fifty-six-year-old Ahmad Abu Asaad, a neighbor of mine. Since our building is still standing, he calls me to ask if he can use the solar panels on our roof to recharge his cell phone each day. I give him permission, and he is welcomed by my sister Samya and her husband, who live at my place now, after theirs was destroyed. Abu Asaad has set up a tent next to the ruins of his home; he and his family are counting on getting help from the neighbors who remain. "We rely on them for the use of their lavatories." He has two reasons to stay, he tells me: "After the truce, Israel will extend their military operations to the South. Though it's difficult now, in the North the worst is over." It's true that some things are starting to function again. The Indonesian Hospital has reopened, thanks to the supply of fuel they received. Al-Shifa Hospital too, even though its director, Mohamed Abu Salmiya, has been arrested, falsely accused of supporting Hamas (in April, he will be released and the charges dropped). Al-Shifa has rebooted its services and even reopened its dialysis center. Movement remains impossible, however, and there's no fresh food to be found. "We still have a lot of canned goods, but getting any potable water remains a challenge," he tells me, signing off.

His fears are not unfounded. First extended for an additional four days, the truce does not hold. Bombing begins again punctually, on the first of December, and by that evening more than a hundred have been killed. On the morning of the 2nd, leaflets fall again on Khan Yunis. They're ordering us to move again, toward Rafah, the southernmost area on the border with Egypt. The flyers have printed maps subdividing the Strip into dozens of small, enumerated blocks. We'll need to keep these maps and memorize them, because from time to time the army will announce, with little advance warning, where to go. Imagining this future is terrifying. How will families with small children and seniors all manage to move out rapidly when they have no means to do so?

The house we're staying in, on the northeast side of Khan Yunis, borders on the last evacuated zone; only the Salah al-Din Road lies between us and them. So we hurriedly put together a plan for relocating to Rafah. We want to be ready, rather than risk acting at the last moment in panic. We decide how to proceed: men and women on foot, children and the elderly in cars. Other families are also making such plans. But no one knows where to go. Many choose the UNRWA tent city on the beach. Next to the sea, however, you're exposed to the cold and humidity. "At least there we'll have food," one person tells me—a reference to the people on the beach who cast their lines into the water, hoping to catch fish. It's a time of chaos. The police have once again disappeared from the streets. Stores are not under assault, though, since there's little left to loot. But there is theft. One robber gets caught; he's beaten and then set free. Without police, turning him in is impossible.

# Rafah

**On the morning of December** 3, the usual leaflets inform us that the eastern part of the city is the next target and should be evacuated immediately. On the subdivided map, zone 42—where we are—also appears. After the warning, a tremendous round of carpet-bombing follows. We are deeply frightened and spend the night packing up our things. Moving a group of twenty-six people, bringing along everything they need—including blankets, mattresses, food, heavy clothing—isn't easy.

Behind my car, we hook up a trailer overloaded with household furnishings. We get it running with cooking oil, since we don't have enough gas. Our neighbors, looking miserable, say goodbye. "We have six elderly people who can't be moved," they tell us, throwing their hands in the air. They'll stay.

We don't know where to go. We spend a night in a house on the outskirts of Khan Yunis because the bombs are falling nonstop. Only the following day do we reach Rafah, where we find shelter in a warehouse put at our disposition by the family of an acquaintance, Hassan Abu Libda. It's in the Al-Salam quarter, near the so-called Philadelphia corridor, the nearly nine-mile-long buffer zone between Gaza and Egypt. Hassan welcomes us there generously. He and his family quickly clean out the space; they give us water to wash with and set up a small bathroom. They refuse to be paid in exchange. But the solution is temporary; he has already given one floor of his house to another family, and our group is far too numerous.

Saeed is the one who finds us an alternative. The Hajezi family agrees to accept our whole group—yes, including us, who are only the friends of their friends. For us, they open up their home in a block of four apartments, where four brothers live with their families; they offer us one floor of the building. I will stay in the basement, with the other two bachelors. The family owns a large plot of land that includes some greenhouses. They grow vegetables and sell them at the local market. How's that for luck? At their house, there's always plenty of food. And they produce electricity as well, thanks to their solar panels. We thank them by buying two 120-gallon barrels of water that cost us sixty dollars, and mules carry them back to our new home.

It's not easy to get cash. We still have some, because in Khan Yunis I was still able to get my salary sent via Western Union. But then the last kiosk where you could get money transfers was destroyed, so that system no longer works. In Rafah, there are still two ATMs. But they only work sporadically, and to withdraw money you need to wait in line for days, with no guarantee that the machine won't run out of cash. Still, there is money in circulation.

In effect, the reopening of the Rafah crossing means that private merchandise begins to be imported again. Everyone already in business begins making huge profits. I manage to get money from a few vendors; I make a deposit with my credit card, which still works perfectly, and they give me the same sum in cash—though not without skimming off their cut. At first, they take 5 percent. Then, little by little, it rises to 25 percent. And storekeepers are cautious. To convince them to sell you flour, you have to be introduced by someone they know and show that you have the money. For the black market price, of course. Fifty-five pounds of flour now costs 300 shekels—over eighty dollars; just a week ago, it sold for fifteen. For people with nothing left, who have already sold their last change of clothing, this price is impossible. For them, the only alternative is aid from UNRWA or the Red Crescent, which have warehouses patrolled by armed guards to prevent looting. They distribute boxes with provisions sized to the number of dependents in need of food. Once home, these small portions have to be rationed; aid consignments are given out only one day a week.

Rafah used to have 200,000 inhabitants: in two days, a million more arrive. The streets are full of people who find no shelter at all, who end up simply dumping their mattresses on the streets; for a roof, they stretch out blankets on poles. Everyone is looking for food, but there's never enough. Even the famous local fish market is empty because the Israeli navy has starting shooting at fishing boats to prevent Hamas militants from retreating by sea. Since then, no one has risked taking their boats out.

It begins to rain. The people camping in the streets don't even look for cover—there's no room. New people have been arriving continually ever since the army ordered all of Khan Yunis to hit the road. Rafah is bursting. The health care situation becomes tragic immediately. There is only a single emergency room, which is already on the point of collapsing. Meanwhile, the air raids strike here as well—houses hiding Hamas militants, the Israelis say. It's a crap shoot. No one can know who is sheltered nearby, or where the bombs will fall next.

I marshal all my ability for persuading to convince my friend Mohammed, with his wife and four children, to leave Khan Yunis. "I don't have anyone who will take me in. Where should I go?" he asks. He knows that the generosity shown early on has been exhausted. People are no longer welcoming strangers into their home; they're afraid someone might be a Hamas fighter in hiding, and their house will turn into a target. I make a lot of calls and finally find a room for Mohammed and his family. They make the move. A few hours later, he phones me, in tears.

"Our apartment was bombed. If you hadn't convinced me to leave, we'd all be dead."

An Israeli official on the radio states that, for every Hamas militant killed, there are two dead civilians. He calls them "collateral damage"—"not a bad average," he adds. His arithmetic of death doesn't add up. For weeks, I've been witnessing entire families buried under the rubble, children torn apart, women killed. Already 18,000 dead, according to the UN. The ratio of two to one just doesn't work.

In the meantime, sporadic violence occurs. A truckload of mineral water is stopped, the driver beaten, and the cargo is stolen. At the crossing, there is tension too. Only ambulances carrying the gravely wounded are allowed to pass, and every opening and closing of the gates is accompanied by a thousand precautions. On the other side, we see Egyptian soldiers with rifles raised.

A sense of guilt nags at me. When I came to the Hajezi family's home, I said nothing about my profession. We journalists are a potential target for Israeli attacks, but when we first arrived, I was so exhausted and confused that I didn't want to risk getting my daughters and me sent away. Such things had already happened to others. One of my colleagues had been shown the door, along with her daughter, by a family who had welcomed her in; they were afraid to let her stay with them any longer. The Hajezis, moreover, are terrified of strangers. Whenever someone comes to visit, they get apprehensive and ask, "Who is he, and what does he do? Do you know him well? Do you know his family?" I'm obligated to tell them who I am and respect their decision. I can't keep making phone calls for work in secret, hiding my PRESS jacket in my car, and putting it on only once I'm far away.

Finally, one morning I decide to confess. I approach the elderly head of the family, pour him a glass of tea, and come clean. "I haven't told you everything about me …" He listens to me. Then he says, "You won't be sent away from my home for this. I have faith. Our fate is written in heaven. You won't be the one who determines ours. We must face the choices of God, not those of men." I feel relieved, and his attitude toward me actually becomes more cordial. As a journalist, I have access to WhatsApp groups where I exchange information with my colleagues. Everyone begins asking me what's happening, and so, each night I become the evening news. The rest of the time, though, we talk about lighter subjects; it's the best way to get some distance from the horror surrounding us. We tell family stories to the youngest kids, recycle gossip, recount the adventures of our ancestors.

Whenever there's network service, my girls spend all their time on their phones. Using WhatsApp, they text their friends and fellow students at the university where they were both enrolled. Bisan majored in information technology, and Ruba was in a nursing program. Unfortunately, the responses they get just raise their level of anxiety. By text message, they find out that one of the girls they were closest to is dead. They cry for days.

The connection is too weak to stream the Spanish Netflix films that my daughters really love, not even their favorite series, *House of Cards*. Their lives are upside-down. They aren't playing their violins, since I made them leave them home. They can't go horse riding—the pastime that helped them get over Bisan's trauma. They're always inside, since it's too dangerous to go out. So, they keep busy helping in the kitchen and taking care of the children staying with us.

I try to teach them not to use hateful language. And not to think in terms of factions, but instead in terms of rights. I tell them that their duty is to live a worthy life. I want to get them out of here. I've already started to ask for help from my network of acquaintances abroad. But it's not easy. Just the same, I do speak to them about it, promising they'll have a normal future, because I want to keep their hopes up. We speak together in English; the language will be useful for them. They smile at all my plans.

## *Silence*

**By now we've learned:** when the networks go dark, Israel is perpetrating some form of horror. From December 15–17, the phone lines are down. Left in that silence, thoughts of my family tear me apart. We're scattered all over: my sister in Jabalia, my parents in Deir al-Balah, my other brother, like me, here in Rafah. I feel blind and deaf with no news from them. Isolated like this from the world outside, I can't even work. I do what I can to stay clear-headed and cheer up the spirits of others.

On one of those horrific nights, a building near the center of Rafah is hit, a few hundred yards from us. The size of the explosion is surprising; it shakes everything. The kids wake up and start to cry. All the windows shatter. It's terrible. Some of the apartments collapse, and the victims are nearly all women and children.

When we get our phones back, the news fills us with horror. In those three days of isolation, dozens of civilians were killed, and the Strip was ravaged from the North to Khan Yunis. The biggest atrocity occurred in the courtyard of Kamal Adwan Hospital. Tents full of the wounded were crushed by tanks; they rolled through, killing patients who were unable to flee. Immediately after, bulldozers plowed over the massacre, burying some who were still alive, according to the testimony of eyewitnesses. At Khan Yunis, the maternity ward of Nasser Hospital was hit; newborns are among the victims. Bombs are again dropped on Al-Shifa Hospital in Gaza City: dozens of deaths. A savage attack on already brutalized Jabalia kills 110 people. The army explains itself once more: these were strategic objectives.

I finally get news from Jabalia. My sister's family is safe, but they're trapped inside their home. There are Israeli snipers in position, ready to shoot. Outside their windows, they see only the bodies of civilians left lying in the street.

In the days that follow, the situation returns slowly to the norm of these abnormal times. The amount of aid increases, and we find a bit more to eat. Water remains the real problem, because the latest bombing did major damage to the hydraulic infrastructure. Everyone survives by inventing some small business or other. They all sell something; most common is homemade food sold in the street by children. Those with nothing sell UNRWA canned-goods vouchers or hawk the contents of their packets directly.

Then there's another blackout, forty-eight hours long, on December 20–21. The number of dead is massive: 390, with 700 wounded. Another terrible bombardment strikes Rafah; the Ali Ibn Abi Talib mosque and the neighborhood around it are destroyed. Bombs also fall on Kuwait Hospital, the place where we journalists convene; some colleagues are wounded. We discover that the attacks no longer target only the living. The cemetery of Gaza City, one of the oldest, has been run over by tanks. They've forced open tombs, bringing bodies to the surface. The umpteenth insult to our local culture—we have deep respect for the deceased. They want to leave us with no reason at all to return. Not even our dead. The bombings have become so intense and unpredictable that the army schedules us a window for going outside. We can leave our homes only for four hours a day, from 10:00 to 2:00. Obviously not enough time to get to the aid stations, wait in line, and make it back home.

# *The Last Beach*

"I THOUGHT THAT KHAN YUNIS was hell because I hadn't been to Rafah." A man camping on the beach with his family tells me this; he set up his tent in the sand some days ago. At night, drafts blow through it from every angle, but sheltering by the sea was his only option, since there was no space left in the city. He tells me about another awful choice he had to make: he received only one UNRWA voucher for winter clothing, which he gave it to his oldest son, who is now the only one with an overcoat, while the rest are freezing. I meet another, even more desperate man. He searched in vain for somewhere his family could stay. He found nothing, and now he's heading back to Khan Yunis. He says, "Better to die at home than in the street."

In Rafah, it keeps getting colder. And we're all very hungry. I notice that there are many once-rich people in the lines for aid. The war erases social hierarchies. I spot Ahmad, a very well-off businessman. He tells me how he'd rented a very big apartment in Rafah, paying 14,000 shekels per month, over $3,800, almost like New York. He's lucky to have such a big home for his family, but their food supplies have run out. There's so little left that even people with money can't find anything to fill their stomachs. On the beach, the SUVs and Mercedes parked in front of some tents are a picture worth a thousand words. They belong to people who, despite ample economic means, couldn't get out of the country when the war began. They rented luxury villas in Khan Yunis and didn't leave in time. When they finally moved to Rafah, the apartments were all taken already. There are no hotels, because there's never been a tourist industry. They had to set up something on the beach, with somewhat more solid tents, though, because they have money to buy wood and nylon.

In the tent cities, a social divide is very easy to see. The tents of the poor are made from fabric and branches, where the cold comes in without knocking. Those of the rich are better; sectioned off into at least three rooms, they're protected by yards of heavy, transparent plastic. Parked in front is their last sign of wealth—expensive cars that no longer take them anywhere.

We're suffering, but in the tent cities, the conditions are definitely worse. There's no privacy. Everyone sees everything that happens, from physical needs to childbirth. And their children are starting to run wild. Kids are wandering off, running risks, infecting each other; they're stealing things, they're disappearing.

*In Rafah, the struggle to survive famine.*

Overall, the situation is getting increasingly tense; it often spills over into violence. People are more aggressive because they see no end to this hell. Everyone is impatient. In the lines outside the UNRWA warehouses, fights break out. The youngest and strongest men—convinced that waiting in orderly fashion leads nowhere—attack the aid trucks more and more often. They feel more shame at their sisters' hunger than they do at becoming thieves. In the morning, their mothers warn them, "Don't come back empty-handed." No one intervenes to stop them, which is no surprise. Israel has bombed the police stations, and the officers are afraid to be seen. They know they're targets.

For days, we find no bread to put on the table. We eat rice given some flavor by a few tomatoes that cost three times what they did last week.

In the evening, we hear about Biden's criticism of Netanyahu and the UN vote for a ceasefire. We're happy, but it's not enough to stop Israel. From the North, I get some terrible news. "They made us leave the school where we found shelter to see if militants were hiding there," one of my uncles still in Jabalia tells me. "They made all the young men strip, then zip-tied and arrested them. Next, they destroyed the school, so now we have nowhere to go."

## *Christmas and New Year's*

I'M SECULAR. I'VE NEVER BEEN an observant Muslim, despite coming from a religious family. But both my daughters and I have always liked seeing the lights on the Christmas tree decorated by the Christians each year in the courtyard of the YMCA. People who don't know Gaza might find this strange, but in a territory with only about six hundred Christians, thousands of people usually participate in Christmas services. I've often gone with my daughters to the mass on Christmas Eve, to celebrate the holiday that our Catholic friends love. We even have a special holiday dinner, featuring pasta with chicken. Yes, pasta—in Gaza, as in nearby Egypt, pasta is part of our regular diet. We season it with chickpeas and lentils, along with a tomato-based sauce.

This Christmas, instead of the shooting star of Bethlehem, we have missiles from Israel. For that matter, the war definitely hasn't spared the Christians; the community in Gaza has been hit along with all the rest. On October 19, eighteen of them died under the rubble of the Greek Orthodox church, Saint Porphyrius. On December 16, a woman and her daughter were killed by Israeli snipers inside the compound of the Catholic community's Holy Family Church. The attack was even condemned by Pope Francis, who from that day on called the sisters there every evening. Bombs also fell on the Orthodox Cultural Center—and on the only Christian hospital in the Strip, Al-Alhi Hospital, originally Baptist and now run by the Anglican diocese. The world is celebrating, but here there's nothing

*Attack on the Baptist Hospital.*

reminding us that this land is said to be holy. The present moment consists of additional evacuations: a new order is directed at the 300,000 residents of Nuseirat. The attacks began just as they were beginning to leave. Eighteen were killed; at that point, it should be no surprise that many others refused to leave. Why go, if you're going to be killed anyway?

During the night between the 24th and 25th, while the world celebrates the birth of Jesus, we are the victims of a new round of bombings. Air raids hit Al-Maghazi and Al-Bureij, in the middle of the Strip; two hundred are killed. Artillery fire is even directed at the central headquarters of the Red Crescent in Deir al-Balah, where there are storehouses with humanitarian aid, a small hospital, a parking area for ambulances, and a hostel for refugees with 15,000 people inside. If the Israelis have reached the point of attacking the headquarters of the organization that helps them with hostage exchanges, in an area where there has never been violence, it means they'll surely been moving their operations here as well. The intensity of the attack worries me; my parents are in that zone.

We begin to lose hope for the wounded, even those that adequate treatment could save. An agreement is signed to medevac out the most severe cases. There are even places ready to receive them, such as the Italian hospital ship *Vulcan*, docked at the Egyptian port of Al-Arish, in the Sinai, less than thirty miles from the Rafah crossing. A lucky few are already there, but the list gets longer each day. There are at least 3,000 severe cases that urgently need to be transported elsewhere. Permits to let them leave, however, are only granted in dribs and drabs; Israel takes the time to decide each case individually. At most twenty leave each day. Many die while waiting.

I have a young cousin on the list; he was wounded in the legs and back. They transported him from the Indonesian Hospital to the Rafah crossing in order to get him out. His fate is uncertain, the doctors say. The fate is similar for the elderly and the chronically ill; the medicine they need is impossible to find. So many deaths are indirectly caused by the war.

The number of refugees in Rafah continues to increase. By now we're a million and a half, with the addition of the evacuees from Nuseirat. The flow of aid, however, is slowing. For weeks now, we have only beans and onions to eat; you can still find them at the market, because they stay fresh longer. Everyone has stomach problems.

In the meantime, the umpteenth blackout cuts off phone connections from 3:00 PM on the 26th until midday on the 27th, hours during which Israel bombs Khan Yunis incessantly. The tremors can be felt even here, ten miles away. The headquarters of the Red Crescent is targeted again. They use drones to shoot at refugees. Twenty-five people die, in the very place where they believed they were safest.

Freezing rain lashes the Strip, bringing a situation already at the limit to utter desperation. At the same time, getting vital goods into Gaza is becoming increasingly difficult. The soldiers impose three levels of inspection, coming and going, and, without any clear reasons, they lengthen the list of products that are prohibited and must therefore be off-loaded at the Rafah crossing. These measures slow the process down to the point of exasperation, creating confusion and long lines of vehicles.

Inside the Strip, the attacks on aid trucks become more and more frequent. Prices continue to rise, but no one has any cash, and the few products you do find at the market sit there unsold. There's a shortage of bread. At first flour was distributed to the bakeries; now they're all closed, and flour goes directly to families. Even so, we've been in line for three days, taking turns every four hours. So far, we haven't gotten a single sack.

A new shipment of propane canisters arrives. On the other hand, again there's no more gasoline. You can only find it on the black market, and now a gallon costs over fifty dollars, where before it was selling for less than eight. Everything again shuts down: the water pumps, the sewer system. Soon this year will end.

It takes us three days to obtain a voucher for a box of aid to feed our family, which has grown in size by New Year's Eve. On the 31st, as a matter of fact, new goods do appear at the market. It's clear some dealers have hidden what they had in order to sell it later for more money. A pound of apples costs almost five dollars, sugar costs nearly four. In the end, our New Year's "feast" consists of beans, canned meat, and dry rusk.

So that's how we finish off a bitter year. I can't remember any that were worse. Everyone is saying that 2023 will mark the end of Gaza. Too many friends and relatives have died atrocious deaths—so many that we don't mourn them anymore. The cities are destroyed. When we meet in the street, we say to each other, "Hope you live through 2024."

Some people simply won't make it. Less than a hundred yards from where we're staying, on the final day of the year, a house with twenty-seven people inside is hit. It's hard to say if this was a targeted attack or a stray bomb. None of us knows that family, the Edwans.

They arrived from the North just three days ago. They are all dead except for Mariam, a thirteen-year-old. I see her taken out from the rubble. While they work on freeing her feet, she's huddled over. Her skin is gray, the color of dust, and she cries silently. Seeing that young girl, the last survivor of her family, touches me. I know her fate has been shared by many others, but she was only a few yards away—it could have been one of my daughters. I wish a better future for Ruba and Bisan, and for all the many Mariams who survive. For all the boys and girls of Gaza.

Despite everything, we decide to celebrate and stay up until midnight, to remember marvelous years as well as sad occasions. In Gaza, we've always welcomed in the New Year by crowding into restaurants and beachside cafés. Despite past attempts by the authorities to restrict festivities, under the idea that sobriety is Islamic, even if no one respects that rigidly here. And in fact, at some point, they gave up. The New Year in 2009, we remember, also began under the bombs. Back then, though, at least we were at home.

# JANUARY

## *Life with No Colors*

**No one goes to Friday** services at the mosques anymore. It's too dangerous. All religious buildings have either been destroyed or may be in short order. We pray at home. On this day of rest, we do still get together; we gather around the radio to listen to the news. There is fighting at the border with Lebanon and tensions inside the Netanyahu government. We don't want there to be a war against Hezbollah, the Shi'ite militants in Lebanon. The army would only end up attacking the Strip even more violently. We're hoping, nonetheless, that disagreements within the administration will lead to the fall of the Netanyahu government and a solution for Gaza.

In the Strip—now divided in two—those in the North have been left in a trap. It's impossible to get out from there, and even simple survival is extremely difficult. Meanwhile, Israel has designated the entire eastern side of Gaza a military zone; no one is allowed to remain. The bottom line is that still more people pour into Rafah, where, however, the humanitarian aid does not increase, so the situation gets worse.

I go to the Tel-al-Sultan camp in search of news, where I meet Basel Al-Maqusi, a very well-known Gazan painter. The last time I saw him was at the opening of one of his exhibitions. "I was living in Beit Lahia, in the extreme North," he tells me. "After October 7th, I understood immediately that my village, so close to the border, would become a target. And so, with my wife and my four children, we left that very day. For a while we were guests at the Window for

Professionals Foundation, an artists' residence where I had exhibited several times. It was close to Al-Shifa Hospital: after the heavy attacks there a month ago, like you we were forced to evacuate to the South."

He didn't find anywhere to stay in Rafah. Now he's in a tent built with nylon and wood, and he and his family are barely surviving. "The rain has soaked through all our possessions—blankets, clothing, food." His youngest children, eight and ten years old, are sick and malnourished. They suffer from constant diarrhea and skin rashes. When he tried to take them to Rafah's Kuwaiti Hospital, "they didn't have the right medicine, so they sent us away."

Everything he has ever painted has been destroyed. But he still wants to keep painting. He found paper and pencils in the Rafah Library, and he is drawing on sheets of paper that he always keeps with him, to protect them from the rain. When he shows them to me, I realize how much his style has changed. Before the war, he composed large, very brightly colored canvases. Now his hand seems tentative, the colors dull. He sketches only planes and rubble, shaded in gray. "That's what I see: death, destruction, fear." He's now working as a volunteer, getting a group of children, ages eight through fifteen, to paint. "Helping them to express their own pain on paper is all I can do for them."

## *Hope from South Africa*

"We're in Phase 3 of the war," announces Yoav Gallant, the Israeli minister of defense. "The army will move from a phase of intense engagement to new types of special operations." To us on the ground, however, the new phase seems dreadfully similar to both the initial aerial phase and the subsequent ground invasion; civilians continue to be targeted with no explanation of the reason behind the attacks. From the crossing point, little aid is coming in, and few wounded are getting out. Hospitals are stretched to the limit. We have no food or water, and gas now costs two hundred dollars a gallon. Too much. At this point, to do my job, I'm forced to get around on foot. I see and know less than before. The unreliability of the phone lines doesn't help, either. I have trouble getting news firsthand.

In this helpless torpor, we learn about the charge of genocide that South Africa has filed at the International Court of Justice in the Hague. We are grateful to this African country. If this really helps us get back home, some of us promise to fly the South African flag over our doors. We're well aware that when the case for international justice against the authors of this genocide was filed, it came not from any Arab nation, our brothers in faith and blood, but from a people who have experienced apartheid and know what oppression and ghettos really are. "Hard to imagine they'll succeed in getting us justice," people are saying, shaking their heads. Yet we grasp at the hope, that the court might at least succeed in imposing extraordinary measures capable of putting an end to the brutality of this conflict.

We listen to the closing statements of the South African lawyers on the radio. They explain, in detail, why what is happening qualifies as genocide: the deliberate elimination of a people locked up in a cage from which there is no escape. We listen to raw, horribly real numbers. There have already been 23,000 dead in Gaza. Each day, two hundred children are killed, forty-three mothers, and three doctors. From inside the cage, however, we see much more than those numbers. Beyond our bodies, they are killing our minds and our hearts, turning us into barbarians. How else can you explain the horror of a man who, unable to bear seeing his own children sleeping on the street in the cold, takes a pistol and kills an entire family so that he can put his own in their tent? Perhaps an isolated incident, this serves as an atrocious sign of the insanity of these times. Violence, after all, by now permeates even the most simple, everyday acts. In the street I live on, there's a bakery where you have to get in line well before 5:00 AM to have a hope of getting anything. And that long line of people is turning into a site of ferocious arguments. Gazans—ever more hungry and angry—have quickly gone beyond fistfights and now use weapons. There are many ways to eliminate a people.

When we hear the Israeli lawyers speak during the same proceedings, we listen to them say that sufficient food is getting into Gaza, that, if anything, "UNRWA isn't up to the task of distributing it." Even so, the numbers speak for themselves: less than 5 percent of the basic daily necessities are being brought in. They've pressed together almost two million people in the South, so many that we'll slaughter each other for a piece of bread, but according to them it's simply a logistical problem. In the courtroom, Israel also rehearses the massacre it suffered three months ago. I don't put the dead on a balance sheet; each death merits equal respect. But here, too, it's civilians who are dying, not the militants responsible for that horrible crime.

For this reason, the South Africans are correct: this is no armed conflict, it's a form of collective punishment. The Israelis have extremely sophisticated technology. They certainly have the capacity for selective targeting. Instead, they've decided to kill indiscriminately. Each day, two million Palestinians are eyewitnesses to their crimes here in Gaza. I, the journalist Sami al-Ajrami, am an eyewitness. And I see not only the physical elimination of individuals but also suffering inflicted with fury on people who are already barely able to survive. Israel keeps the border closed; it starves us by allowing aid in as it pleases. It punishes everyone, children included, for horrors committed by others. One simple statistic demonstrates this: during the hearings, there were twelve more bombings, 126 killed, and 241 wounded.

Children are the weakest link in this war. It's enough to look at the numbers released by Save the Children. In less than one hundred days, ten thousand have died. In the dark art of bookkeeping, however, the number of disappeared under the rubble goes missing: 4,000 young lives, lost. Those who survive are facing a grim reality; thousands have suffered amputations, and there are orphans everywhere. They beg on the streets, or they stand there, listless and silent. They're all getting sick because there's no potable water. They don't eat enough, and they have no clothes to protect themselves from the cold. They are the victims of unspeakable traumas; often you see it when they draw pictures—airplanes with monster faces, spitting fire. A people also can be eliminated by annihilating its children, the seed of its future.

Even the granddaughter of my sister Samya (the daughter of her son), Nejwa, is in the "Indonesian" hospital up north. With a head wound, she risks losing an eye. The hospital in Gaza City that specializes in ophthalmology has been destroyed; nowhere else is capable of treating her, and only abroad will they be able to save her sight. I think about her when I pass by the Kuwait Hospital, where there is a long line of women squeezing in their arms the small, suffering bodies of their sick or wounded children. They're waiting to be assigned a space, often just some corner on the floor, where at least they'll be treated. I slip into the jam-packed rooms of the pediatric ward, and, when I see the horrible conditions these little ones endure, I feel an impulse to vomit.

The country of South Africa that defends us today has seen dark days, yet it managed to find truth and justice. Who knows if, for us, the hour of truth and justice will ever arrive?

## *Nothing That Moves Forward*

**A NEW COMMUNICATIONS BLACKOUT SILENCES** the voices of Gazans from January 13–20, for eight full days—the longest disruption since the start of the war. To get any news I'm forced to go far from my house, until I reach a zone where you can connect to the Egyptian network. In this area, a man has fashioned something of an internet café, setting up plastic chairs in front of his home. At the modest price of one shekel per hour (about twenty-seven cents), he'll let you connect to his Egyptian network card. It's the only way I can manage to find out what is happening around us and how close the fighting is. Walking that route, it takes me three hours a day to get there and back. All around I see people shattered by the lack of connection to their loved ones; many are simply sitting on the ground, doing nothing at all. It reminds me that none of us thought to bring books with us, and now we have little or nothing to read. I think about what I miss most from my library at home, and I can't decide between Fyodor Dostoevsky and Jean-Paul Sartre. I opt for the Frenchman. I could use his blunt words to make sense of my nausea.

What I read on my phone surpasses my wildest imagination. Israel bombed the satellite dishes of PalTel, the Palestinian telephone network, and when the technicians arrived to make repairs, the army shot at them as well. Two workers are dead; two others are gravely wounded. I also find out—just as happened already in Gaza City—that the Khan Yunis cemetery has been desecrated. They used tanks to destroy tombs and trample the dead. Officially, the purpose was to assure there were no Hamas tunnels under the coffins. This time the Israelis even went so far as to exhume the most recently buried bodies, at least twenty-one of them. They've brought them to Israel to verify that there are no hostages among them. When they didn't find any, they brought them back and left them where they found them. Without burying them, though.

During the silence, 165 people died, most of them killed in the area around Nasser Hospital and around the general headquarters of the Red Crescent in Khan Yunis. There are 208 wounded.

We deal with the silence by gathering together around the fire. We drink tea along with the dry rusk from the humanitarian aid packets; in the evenings, we turn on the radio, making use of batteries that we continually move from one contraption to another. That's how we learn about the umpteenth attempt by Qatar to secure an agreement for a ceasefire. At the same time, the youngest in our group want to follow the games of the European soccer championship or the Egyptian league, so they can then debate animatedly the merits of various coaches and players—and focus on something far away from the war.

Only after a week of negotiations does the Palestinian phone company reach an agreement with the army and repair the network. When the lines are back up, I find out that they've disconnected us in an even more significant fashion: they've literally erased our existence in the present along with our past. They had already bombed archaeological digs, mosques, and ancient churches. During the last long eight days, they also razed the public registry office to the ground. The process of digitalizing records had just begun; so many documents were paper and still in file cabinets. The bombardment destroyed all the birth and death certificates, so we no longer have anything that attests to our existence. We can only rely on whatever we've carried with us. It's a real problem. I meet one boy who just lost his identity card; in order to get him a new one, the police want a copy of the one that's been lost. But he doesn't have it.

Earlier bombings of the university and the Ministry of Education had burned up a large part of student exam records as well as their degree certificates. If they didn't take their records with them when they fled, how will they be able to show they have their degrees? Even the courthouse no longer exists. When it burned, thousands of official acts burned with it. The same is true of property records. I already know that when the war is over, it will be a challenge to show who owns homes and land parcels. Many people believe this is the clearest sign of Israeli's intention to bring settlers back to Gaza.

## *Twenty-one Soldiers*

**An action claimed by Hamas** kills twenty-one Israeli soldiers—young reservists—just six hundred yards from the Israeli border. The army spokesperson, Daniel Hagari, announces the killings, describing it as "the most serious incident involving our soldiers since the beginning of the war." They were killed by an antitank missile launched at a building that the soldiers were preparing to blow up, adds Hagari, "in the attempt to establish a buffer zone that would allow Israeli residents living in proximity to the Strip to return to their homes."

Some people hope that the grief suffered by these soldiers' families will bury Netanyahu. After all, didn't the hostages' families barge into the Knesset? Maybe this government is showing a few cracks at last, they say. The pessimists—the majority (and I'm one of them)—believe that the twenty-one fallen soldiers will simply cause more deaths. The news that follows confirms this. According to the Israelis, the Hamas leadership is locked down in Khan Yunis. I don't know if this is true, but I hardly expect the militants to give themselves up. Even if they came out with their hands up, they'd be killed anyway, and they know it. And, in fact, they do reject the two-month truce offered by Israel in exchange for all the hostages. Khan Yunis, as a result, is surrounded, and the entire Nasser Hospital compound is targeted. In short order, it is filled with corpses. The wounded are left lying in agony in the street because snipers keep the ambulances from reaching them.

In any case, the real motor of political change ought to be the Gazan population. If the anger we feel carried the day, the movement would be finished. I hear it now constantly: "Enough with Hamas!" Before, no one would have dared to say it.

News broadcasts are discussing the negotiations led by Qatar. By this point, however, it's difficult for us to believe that anything concrete will come from these talks; every day the war gets more and more savage. The dead, the hunger, the violence are slowly swallowing us up. My sister Samya tells me how people in the North have begun eating pet food and tree leaves, since they have nothing else. We're barely surviving. And we have to count ourselves lucky; in Khan Yunis, intense military operations are continuing. There are at least twenty different bombardments with victims.

The western part of the city—where 14,000 refugees live in tents set up outside the general headquarters of UNRWA—is attacked by artillery fire; there are fourteen dead and eighty wounded. Perhaps more, since rescue teams weren't allowed in. In the meantime, the headquarters of the Red Crescent is again hit, along with the area around Nasser Hospital, which has been besieged by tanks for days.

In Rafah, chaos erupts. There are protests against everything. You hear people yelling, "A curse on Israel!" and "Hamas be damned!" Everyone is furious at the militants. They confiscate medicine from the humanitarian aid and resell it on the black market. In the refugee camps, some of the militants are running around like gangsters, brandishing weapons. They beat or shoot at the feet of anyone who opposes their injustice; they take food and supplies for themselves. But the anger against them is stronger and stronger. For the first time, people scream at them, "Enough of Hamas! You've made us into hostages!"

We're hungry. Beyond the Rafah crossing, though, there's a mile-long line of aid trucks that Israel refuses to grant authorization to enter. They're simply stuck. That's why, when a rare shipment does arrive in the North, all hell breaks loose. The tragedy occurs in Gaza City, where snipers shoot at the thousands of people gathered and awaiting aid in Kuwait Square on the east side of the city. Twenty people die, and another 150 are wounded. According to the army, they were all terrorists, but this isn't true. They were civilians who, in the momentary chaos, got a little too close to the checkpoints. By now we know: Israeli soldiers shoot first and give warnings later. It happens again a few hours later. A family tries to move south, waving a white flag. They get mowed down by machine guns. The army tells us that they didn't follow their instructions quickly enough. They might not even have understood them. Not many here speak Hebrew.

# *Alzheimer's*

I **HAVEN'T SEEN MY PARENTS** for quite a while, so I decide to visit them, even though it's dangerous. I start up the coast road—on foot, since my car's gas tank is empty. I feel guilty staying so far from them. I'm running a great risk by traveling, but my mother has been expecting me for ages now; hugging me again, I hope, will give her the energy to keep on going for a while. The route is difficult, but after two hours I get to Deir al-Balah, where my folks are still staying in my sister's villa, the "chalet," which is increasingly packed with my relatives. They all seem to have aged and lost weight. My father has a serious illness, Alzheimer's. He hasn't been himself for a while now, but the war has made his condition worse. Living so far away from his home, which was his whole life, he's lost. He asks incessantly to be brought back there, dozens of times each day, until my mother and everyone around him are exasperated. He often asks about people who have passed away, some long ago and many only recently, and his questions renew the grief of their relatives. He wants to eat and drink all the time. He's hungry, but he also immediately forgets when he has eaten. He's very difficult to manage.

Only minutes after I arrive there, the Hague Tribunal announces its order for extraordinary measures. Israel will have to allow more aid in and limit its attacks. Good, but not great, since there's no order for a ceasefire. Our disappointment is deep. We aren't unprepared for this result, of course, and we understand why in Ramallah they're celebrating, with Foreign Minister Riyad al-Maliki declaring, "The ruling is in favor of humanity." I'm not unaware of the expansive, long-term implications of this decision. But we're not in the West Bank. We're suffering here and now.

Despite the demands from the Hague, the army imposes yet another forced displacement on Khan Yunis. I leave too. I would like to follow the river of people, but many, I realize, aren't heading to the security of Rafah; instead, they're heading north. "Risking death is better than going to Rafah," they tell me. "It's too full of people; there's no room left, and it's agonizing." The scene is grotesque. Despite the fact that we're well into winter, hundreds of people with lightweight clothing are marching like zombies in the January freeze. There are far too many people on the road; it takes me five hours to make it back. A major storm is on the way, and everyone is working to reinforce their tents against the gale. I see pain everywhere.

The next night, one of the rainiest and coldest of January, an old friend, just arrived from Khan Yunis, knocks at my door. The battles there have become violent, and in the middle of the night the soldiers forced him, his wife, his four children, and his elderly father to leave the tent where they had been living, in what's left of the Al-Maghazi camp. They had no time to take anything with them. He begs me to let him and his family stay. But we're already twenty-six extra people in a building where twenty-eight others were already living. The apartments are more than full already; there just isn't room. I give him some plastic sheeting we'd bought to reinforce windows where bombing has shattered the glass. He's embarrassed and apologizes for disturbing us. He tells me he's knocked on many doors already: no one helped him. This head of a family—forced to make his children sleep on a filthy sidewalk, soaked with rainwater and sewage—cries a long time on my shoulder. But at this point we can no longer even permit ourselves to show human solidarity. Each of us must think solely about the survival of our own family.

The radio announces that Israel has warned Egypt of its intention to invade Rafah, until now the last city spared from heavy battles. They want to take control of the "Philadelphia corridor" along the southern border and conduct military operations right here, in the overcrowded city center—where we too are living. This prospect terrifies us; if Israel attacks Rafah, with the Egyptian border closed, we will have no place left to go. So much for those orders from the Hague; this would be a massacre, announced in advance. No one believes it's a bluff. It's only a matter of time, and the mood is somber. And it doesn't help that many countries have decided to block UNRWA funding, after Israel accused twelve of its employees—though they don't give names—of having participated in the October 7 attacks. If there are people stained with such crimes in its ranks, well then, let them be arrested and tried. But UNRWA has 13,000 employees. It's yet another disproportionate act of collective punishment. Outside of Palestine, perhaps people aren't aware of the UN's role here. Just to give a single example, only in its offices can we find essential sorts of medicine—even more so now that the pharmacies have used up their stock, and we're all getting sick.

I have a job, and I still can manage to get my paycheck. But at least a million and half people are unemployed and don't have a dime left. They survive thanks to the weekly boxes of basic necessities—the blankets and tents distributed by UNRWA—even in the most remote areas. If its employees lose their jobs, the chaos will get even worse than it is. For Palestinian refugees, the UN Relief and Works Agency represents our hope for a future. After each war, we've only rebuilt our homes and hospitals, our schools and universities thanks to the support of the UN. Freezing its funding, floating the idea of letting it die, means killing thousands of Gazan citizens—forgetting that they are civilians, not militants. Gaza citizens endure, in fact, the worst from both sides.

On the radio, Abu Mazen says, "This act is aimed at discrediting UNRWA and getting rid of the refugee question." I fear instead that they want to use their accusations as a pretext for bombing even the UNRWA headquarters in Rafah. They'll say that there are terrorists inside, and why not, since no one will ask them for proof? In this area there are thousands of tents, so many that you can't see the building behind them. It would be a catastrophe.

## *Zombie Land*

**My daughter Bisan is sick.** During the day, I try to find her a bit of privacy, but at night it's impossible. We sleep huddled together. I'm worried; infectious diseases are spreading, and here in Rafah, there are already cases of cholera and perhaps even typhoid. The rain has caused the sewers to overflow, and you can't know what germs you might be bringing home after day of walking in mud and wastewater. We don't have enough water to wash our hands more than once a day. The hospitals are overcrowded and the doctors overburdened, so it's tough to get a diagnosis of what's making you sick.

We just buried a neighbor. She died from disease, and we don't know which. Sadly, many of the elderly pass away like that. I'm afraid for my young and brilliant girls. They've already lost their home, their family, their friends. They're even losing their hopes and dreams. I try to keep up their spirits, telling them about the life they'll have in Europe, but they've stopped believing me. I see them slipping into an apathy that's tearing me apart. They'll get over their illnesses; their bodies will continue to function. But how will they manage to heal from the wounds that this war is inflicting on their minds and their hearts?

After Bisan, five more people in our house fall ill. I'm sick too. It's cold, and we're all worn out. But then at least we do start getting a bit more water. The United Arab Emirates has built a desalination plant west of Rafah, in Egyptian territory, so that we are supplied with more potable water. Unfortunately, it's still very little. We stock up on it, buying some from the tanker trucks every ten days. We store it in barrels, measuring it out, a set amount for each person. They say that even this water is contaminated, due to the amount of damage to the infrastructure, and it may be the major source of infections. There's even a risk of Legionnaires' disease. We boil everything, but we don't know if that's enough.

The news from the radio doesn't help our morale. In Israel, the ex-settlers of Gaza who left in 2005 have organized a conference to discuss how to take back our land. I continue to think that this must be Israel's real plan. In the North, entire villages have been flattened, the farmland has been devastated, and they've exploded all the buildings left standing after the bombing. They don't want to leave us anything to return to. And yet we're so focused on surviving that this isn't even our major concern. We might all die. If it isn't the bombs, it will be starvation or sickness. By now Gaza has become a land of zombies: the weak, the children, the elderly, they all look like the walking dead. They surely won't last long.

I ask everyone, Do you want to stay or go? Before, they used to say that they wanted to die here, at home. Now most have changed their minds. This death is too slow and undignified. "I want to leave," they say. "Leave this horror behind." Starting again somewhere else, we tell ourselves, is the only way to save—even more than our families—our history, our language, our traditions, our memory.

# FEBRUARY

## *Illusions*

**The chocolate has disappeared from** UNRWA food packets. We were giving it to the children—to help them cope with moments of panic during the bombing or to help them get their energy back. With nostalgia, I remember our shatawi, traditional cookies filled with cream and glazed with chocolate. Gaza was famous for its sweets. Taking our kids to the pastry shop on Fridays was a tradition, and we really miss it. Instead, I invent a game: each taking turns, the twelve children staying with us can ask for a special dish or dessert. In the days that follow, we do everything we can to deliver that dish, no matter how little it may resemble what was originally requested. In this way, we give each child a minute or two of normal life, along with the illusion that their wishes can still be fulfilled. Of course, it isn't easy, and the results are often disappointing. But we pretend to be satisfied.

Staying inside is hard for the youngest kids. But they need to stay off the streets and away from kids their age, so they don't get sick. Naturally, they're not happy about it; they want to go outside and get some fresh air. So we try to give them some special moments; we teach them card games, nursery rhymes, and even DIY projects. I've discovered that they love to repair broken toys. Fixing a doll or toy car makes them feel grown up and skillful. We also try to make them responsible, and give them small housekeeping chores, such as setting or clearing the table.

It's hard for the oldest kids too. After Bisan got sick, Ruba was next: fever, bone pain, and a stomachache. It's very cold outside, so we all try to stay home as much as possible. Visiting a doctor is unthinkable, not without spending long, freezing hours in line.

My daughters slowly return to form, and I start hoping again. In the city, too, the atmosphere improves, since they're even talking about a new, six-week truce. We have the feeling that the outside world is trying to make something happen. With such a short window of time, it will be difficult for people from the North like us to get back to our homes. But those from the middle of the Strip might manage; down here, they were the last to arrive, when it was already late, so they were forced to camp on the muddy sidewalks or set up tents on the beach. At least they'll find out if they have anything left, and they'll empty out this overcrowded city. I'm also hoping I can start being a better journalist again. The latest round of bombings and military operations forced me to stay in Rafah, and the view from my balcony shrank; I could see only whatever happened directly around me. With the truce, I will again be able to travel around the Strip to track down stories and witnesses.

With such thoughts, on the evening of February 2, people pour into the streets in joy. "Hamas and Israel have reached an agreement!" they cry. I feel an indescribable sense of relief, not least because the army had earlier announced that, in Khan Yunis, its "work was done," which to my ears sounded like a threat for Rafah.

In just a few hours, Israel strips away our illusions. They're still negotiating; the militants don't want to accept any agreement that doesn't include a permanent ceasefire. A sense of desperation envelops Rafah, mixing with the rain and mud. If Israel decides to attack here as well, where else can we flee? The army wants to move us to the area of Al-Mawasi, the beach west of Khan Yunis, which is already overcrowded with tents. Imprisoning two million people in two square kilometers of shoreline—roughly a mile and a quarter—isn't just crazy, it's cruel.

We hear Jens Laerke, the spokesperson for the UN Office for the Coordination of Humanitarian Affairs, on the radio: "Rafah is a pressure-cooker of despair." Yes, that and a lot more. And when, that evening, the Israelis unleash another round of leaflets on our heads, we really feel we've been taken for a ride. Luckily, it's not the usual evacuation order; instead, it's an invitation to "wake up." In what looks like a two-page newspaper spread, they enumerate the crimes of Hamas for us—as if we needed them to tell us. The leaflets achieve the opposite aim: they make us feel that the militants' horror of Israel is justified. People get angry; they rip them up. To me, it seems that Israel and Hamas need and sustain each other. They keep us civilians in the middle, between them.

## He Was My Father

**My father Mohamed was running** a fever, like everyone in Gaza. They took him to the emergency room late in the evening, but the doctors felt it wasn't serious, and they sent him home. They ought to have admitted him. He died a few hours later, at 2:00 AM on Sunday the 4th. When they called from Deir al-Balah to say that he was very sick, my brother Hassan and I immediately started back along the coast road. It was dark, so we left when it was the most dangerous. We walked quickly, trying to get there as soon as possible, but we arrived too late; he was already dead. The tragedy that struck my family, unfortunately, is all too common in these past months. The war has worn the life out of the elderly. They die from trivial illnesses.

Before he came down with Alzheimer's, my father was a lot of fun, a nice man. He laughed a lot. He was also hypercritical, always a contrarian and ready to face any interlocutor. He criticized the administration of Gaza with cutting remarks; he'd call them "idiots," arguing that they wanted to return us to the Middle Ages. In our family everyone loved him; he was one of our last remaining elders. When his memory was still working, he would be the one to tell our family stories. I loved taking him and my mother to the beach. They'd squabble, and we'd make fun of them. During the whole period of the war, he seemed weak and confused. I saw that he was sad and angry. He wanted to go back home.

I'm very sad. It's sad when you can't take care of your own parents. Or your own kids.

But there's no real time for grief. We must face the hell of bureaucracy in wartime. In the morning, very early, we have to bring him to the hospital to get a death certificate. It's a journey into hell; the morgue is flooded with corpses deposited on the pavement everywhere. We get his papers and deal with the funeral arrangements. In normal times, we would have waited until his closest family members arrived, but obviously that's not possible. There are barely ten of us there to say goodbye. We pray in an area next to the hospital, but while we're in line, waiting for a melancholy ceremony, the final cleansing of the body, bombs begin to fall nearby. We have to interrupt the funeral and look for shelter. It all takes an hour longer than expected.

Thanks to my brother's contacts at the Red Crescent, we at least manage to organize transport for the body in an ambulance to the cemetery. We're privileged compared to so many others, who are forced to load the bodies of their loved ones on gurneys dragged by donkeys.

Or, in the best case, in the back of a pickup. But we are forced to dig a grave for him by ourselves in the space left between those of his relatives.

We go back to the "chalet." Luckily, everyone there is a friend or relative, and we're surrounded with affection and expressions of support. Our mourning ritual traditionally lasts for three days, but we tighten up the schedule and sit with the family to grieve for only twenty-four hours. The situation is too dangerous and unpredictable. Hassan and I are in a hurry to return to our families. My sisters, one of them safe in Saudi Arabia, the other trapped in the area north of the Strip, are sad and angry that they can't be with us. They cry and cry on the phone.

When I get back to Rafah, a great number of friends call to offer their condolences. Usually, friends and colleagues participate in mourning by coming to visit at the house, where we offer them coffee and pastries. For obvious reasons, we're in no position to do that here, so instead I go to meet them in front of the Kuwait Hospital, where we journalists always meet. At least I have some way to thank them.

# *Emergency Plan*

**The radio wakes us up** with more bad news. Netanyahu thunders, "In two days, Rafah will be attacked." The army is ready. Even Egypt is reinforcing its defenses. Evidently, if the Israelis advance this far, the Egyptians are worried about an assault on the border. The prospect is terrifying. We're all anxious and confused.

Our moods are controlled by the news, which doesn't get any better. Israel and Hamas can't come to an agreement. Yet another diplomatic mission by Anthony Blinken, the US secretary of state, has failed. Here we continue to die. These days, when people meet on the street, they greet each other by saying, "Let's hope we're alive tomorrow." The odds of surviving become increasingly tenuous. Whatever gives us hope in the morning disappoints us by nightfall. We go to bed exhausted. More and more openly, we blame everything on Hamas. "Their violence and intransigence are mistakes," I hear people say. But at the same time, people curse the Israeli army, calling them "merciless," "cruel," and "sadistic" for the way they revenge themselves on a bone-weary population.

We can't let them catch us unprepared. We talk things through, calling an assembly that includes everyone except the smallest children. We have to make an important decision, and we have to do it together. Initially, I speculate about going to my sister's "chalet" in Deir al-Balah, where my mother is staying. But there are already three hundred people there, so there's little room. They would certainly welcome in me and my daughters, but not our friends, and we don't want our group to separate; by now we need and depend on each other. The "chalet" becomes my destination of last resort. We'll go there only if we can't avoid it.

The safest solution, however, is also the most difficult. When the evacuation order is given, we'll move to the beach—in Khan Yunis, though, not the overcrowded shoreline here in Rafah. At the moment, Khan Yunis is still a danger zone, but the soldiers will be done exploring every inch of that area before they decide to move south. We inspect the neighborhood there and manage to locate a secluded, almost abandoned area on land owned by the al-Agha family, who hosted us before in Khan Yunis, then came with us to Rafah. We've become a community centered around four nuclear families, almost sixty people. A tribe. We've gotten to know each other well; we get along, and we're efficiently organized in dividing up our chores. We feel safe together.

Of course, it's also arduous terrain. We'll need to prepare well and study every detail. We'll need buy tents or get them made. We'll need to collect rugs and wrap the tents with them to insulate us from the cold. We'll need to decide how to transport and protect our basic necessities: mattresses and blankets, propane tanks and dishes, along with our stock of food and potable water. At the moment there's next to nothing in that area, except an old outhouse that agriculture workers used. We chose that site because the army couldn't possibly imagine any tunnels are there. At the same time, it's not too far away from an emergency room with ambulances. If someone gets sick, it won't be too difficult to get them treated. Our plan goes in the opposite direction from what all the other families are doing in this moment. The tendency is to crowd together near schools or UNRWA storehouses, or else close to the hospitals and headquarters of the Red Crescent. But that's a mistake. By now it's clear that crowded sites don't prevent military actions; on the contrary, since the army is convinced that militants use civilians as shields, such sites are precisely where they do attack.

We begin to prepare. More accurately, our bags are already packed because we never unpacked at Rafah. We change our clothes, taking out what's in the suitcases; after washing what we've been wearing, we pack those up instead. We're always ready to flee. In fact, we all carry everything essential around our neck or waist: identity papers and treasured keepsakes. I carry family photos, my father's watch, and the keys to my house. In her bag, my daughter Ruba carries a letter from her dead cousin. The soldiers with their leaflets will tell us when to leave.

We want to be ready. When it happens, timing will be crucial. You don't want to move a moment too soon or a moment too late. When the crowds fill up the roads, it'll be chaos. Assuming that the usual warnings will be given, of course. They could also decide to isolate us, closing the roads before their attack in order to be sure that not a single Hamas member escapes. In that case, it will be a massacre.

Each of us, therefore, has their duties to fulfill in the shortest time possible. I spend my days with a talented tent-builder and give him precise directions about what we want. Our plan envisages a circus-size tent, large enough to house our entire, sixty-four-member community, along with smaller attached structures so that each family will have some privacy. We've already marked our chosen terrain with wooden stakes and nylon sheets, and now some of us are taking turns sleeping there. To survive in that place, we'll need a good deal of supplies, including a chemical toilet. We stock up on propane tanks and gasoline, some insulating material to put on the ground, and even a woodstove. We find all these things on the black market. We also buy a great deal of food along with first aid and medical supplies. Once we're set up there, we plan to go out as little as possible, at least until this new storm has passed. One remaining problem is communication. There's no network connection, and so, to use a phone, you need to walk a mile and a quarter.

## *Panic*

**These preparations are abruptly interrupted** on February 12 by an attack inside Rafah—very nearby, less than a hundred yards from our home. It's already night when rocket fire lights up the darkness and the din becomes terrifying. The army invades the city, first with planes attacking from the air, then by land, with tanks ushering in special forces. Only the next morning do we learn that this coordinated operation—which also involved Israel's police and the Shin Bet secret service—managed to liberate two hostages. To bring those two men home alive, sixty-seven people were killed.

Israel hasn't given an evacuation order, but this operation in the city center unleashes panic. What if there are hostages hidden in some other anonymous apartment block? They might be anywhere, and when the army attacks, it destroys everything around the hapless hideout. This was meant to be a crucial day for our preparations, but we don't dare to go out. There's too much confusion and fear in the streets.

The raid puts a hitch in our plans. Goods that were available just yesterday disappear in just a few hours—including the wood needed to construct our new shelters. This problem slows us down greatly. I had already agreed on a delivery date with our builder, but now we'll have to rethink everything. There's nothing to be found, except at impossible prices. Even food, propane tanks, and blankets now cost triple. And so, instead of getting a head start for our move, our group finds itself behind the others; the coast road is already crowded with people fleeing toward the center of the Strip. A new raid could happen any minute, and no one wants to take risks.

Some of us would like to leave, though we're still not ready. We can't manage without the equipment; there's nothing set up in our chosen spot, and we have only five of our nine tents. We discuss it all animatedly. In the end, we decide to wait until we've scraped together as much as we need. We do at least work out the logistics for our move. We have to travel four miles in the open, where we'll be vulnerable. The situation is unstable, changing constantly. It's hard to keep a level head, especially when we're all exhausted.

We also have another problem: we're running out of cash. I still have my salary, but I can't withdraw money anywhere or even get it the way I had been, by using a credit card. The percentages they're asking have risen to loan-shark rates: 25 percent. Way too much.

In less than a week, however, by spending everything we have, we manage to find sources for everything we need. Though it isn't easy, we transport by car the wood for structures we'll cover with fabric and plastic. We gather up the food we've found—mostly rice, beans, flour, and sugar—along with some recycled solar panels that we bought and hope to use for generating electricity. For water, we'll use the farm's irrigation system that's already in place.

I drive my overloaded car down the road to Khan Yunis, and it feels like a metropolitan thoroughfare during rush hour. Cars, carts pulled by donkeys, people on bikes or on foot—everyone fleeing, carrying with them the little they have left. Fear of invasion, after all, is worse than an unknown future. Negotiations are at a dead end. The ceasefire is again far off, and a video broadcast by Israel showing Yahya Sinwar—the Hamas leader in Gaza—in the tunnels of Khan Yunis seems yet another signal that the war will continue. I feel very anxious. When we get to our chosen beach, I begin furiously cutting the wooden support beams for our roof, hoping work will distract me. I stare out to sea, trying to lose myself.

## *Birthday Cake*

We set up the tents, putting the recycled solar panels on top of them; we build a chemical toilet and a storage shed, which we fill up with flour. Sacks and sacks of it. And it's thanks to that treasure, the result of painstaking research and tough negotiation, that my girls prepare a surprise for me. I would have bet that February 14, 2024, my fifty-seventh birthday, would be my saddest ever. Instead, at dinner they present me with a small, homemade cake with little pieces of chocolate inside—who knows how they got it. I'm not expecting it, so I get very emotional. I cry. It's a surreal moment of normality: my daughters and friends around me, singing "Happy Birthday" as if we're at home, in our own house, in our old life, in peacetime. I close my eyes, make a wish, and for a long moment I try to forget the war. Who knows how much effort they put into getting that chocolate, I tell myself. It's the best cake I've ever eaten.

Keeping busy rescues me from feeling depressed constantly due to the latest bad news—the deplorable plan of Netanyahu "to rescue" (as he puts it) "the civilians in Gaza before attacking Rafah." Only someone who has never been here could think that makes sense. In truth, this plan is a premeditated crime. He wants to force two million people onto the shore. It's madness: that section of beach is too narrow, there's no room and no facilities of any kind. Among other things, there are no water hydrants, no sewers, and no storehouses for the aid that no one is in charge of managing and distributing. In short, it's all a lie. The Israeli prime minister wants to maintain appearances, asserting that the war continues to follow humanitarian law. But it's exactly the opposite.

The situation pushes Rafah even further into chaos. Crowds assault the crossing point, shouting out anti-Hamas slogans and cursing Sinwar. They burn tires and break through the protective barrier. They don't make it to the border, however; on the other side, the Egyptians have their weapons loaded and are ready to gun them down. The people curb themselves, occupying no man's land for only a few hours. There they find some trucks full of aid that hasn't been distributed; they break into those and loot the supplies. Some do it to feed their families, others to resell it later. The police take their time but eventually intervene. They fire their weapons, and there are some tense moments.

I don't see any of this myself; I was told about it afterward. I'm still on the beach with my group, intent on finishing up our shelter. When we're finally done, four of us stay to protect our supplies. We can't let ourselves be robbed; we've invested everything we have in this campsite.

On the coast road, we run into a gang of young men who stop cars and demand bribes. They want money, food, clothing; you have to give them something to satisfy them. Otherwise, the least that can happen is they break your car windows with stones. Or rob you savagely. They settle for my precious cigarettes and let us go. Gangs are a new phenomenon, a result of the fact that police stations have been bombed, and the officers are more and more disorganized. Public safety is no longer assured.

Today is a Friday, the day of prayer—usually a calm day even during these months of war. Instead, in the street it's utter chaos. The residents of Rafah, the only small city that has thus far been spared from the bombing, know that they have to flee. They're leaving their lives behind them and selling everything they can't manage to carry—clothing, pots and pans, rugs, radios, provisions, solar panels, telephones, car parts. A hellish scene.

## *Going/Staying*

**After long discussions and a** majority vote, we decide to stay in Rafah as long as conditions allow us to do so. In the area near the beach, everything is ready. Our tents are there, our portable toilet, and our provisions, not to mention an armed guard charged with protecting our supplies, since robberies are increasingly common. Still, so long as the soldiers aren't targeting Rafah, it's safer to stay in the city. Here we have access to humanitarian aid, we can buy food at the market, and we have at least minimal medical care available. One more thing, for me, is particularly important. Since there's no internet or telephone networks at the beach, working there will be difficult. I tried to set up a router in one of the tents, but it didn't work. Now that we have everything ready, we can move our little community in three hours or less. In an emergency, we'll manage to get out in time.

In the North, in contrast, things are getting worse. An umpteenth bombardment—this one kills eighty-five people. Water quality continues to get worse, and food is so scarce that people are resorting to livestock grain to appease their hunger. The telephone lines are down, and I can't speak to my sister Samya for days. Rafah becomes more and more chaotic. Armed gangs wander the streets on the city's outskirts and break into empty houses to loot them. Fights start up constantly. One night, a group of men, convinced that someone they were following was coming to our place, charge into our house, ready to beat him. I need all my gift of gab to calm them down and convince them they need to look elsewhere. The police have disappeared, and there's no security. Aid trucks are attacked nonstop, and their drivers are afraid, so they no longer want to come into the city, which makes the already high prices rise even further. I'm afraid too. I would never be able to push someone aside to grab food for myself. We now go to the market in groups of three or four, and we return home quickly.

I want to get my daughters out of the Strip. More terrified all the time, they wail and shake from fear each time a bomb falls. I can no longer calm them. No parent can live with seeing their children experience these conditions, so I ask all my friends abroad—connections I've made through my job—to help me put together enough money to arrange for their departure. Fundraisers are already in progress.

You see, there is a way to get out of Gaza. A system was already in place before the war, and some weeks ago, it started up again. It works, provided you have plenty of money: $5,000 (and it has to be in dollars; they won't take the equivalent in other currencies) per person, and $2,500 for small children. We rely on a travel agency named Hala. For these steep prices, in relatively short order (just two or three weeks), their employees handle all the required bureaucracy, taking advantage of their special access to the Egyptian authorities. If for some reason, the "client" isn't able to leave, they receive a partial reimbursement, "minus the expenses for visa paperwork." In the past, the agency's costs were so low that it steamrolled all its rivals: just $350 was enough to get you out of Gaza. Now its prices have increased tenfold. It costs a bundle, but not so much that it has become impossible, if you have friends and relatives in some foreign country who are ready to help. The application process is simple; you can do it online. And there are various means to make contact, including Telegram and other messaging services.

"If you open the gate tomorrow, more than half the people in Gaza would like to leave," says Scott Anderson, the Director of UNRWA Affairs in Gaza, in a press briefing. And he's right. Israel's systematic destruction of our land, ethnicity, and culture no longer leaves us with any reason to stay.

Whoever applies—and pays—only has to wait until their name appears on the lists of approved travelers. The lists are published at 10:00 PM; by 8:00 the next morning, you already need to be at the border, so there's practically no time for goodbyes. The border inspections are lengthy on both the Palestinian and the Egyptian sides. A luxurious, air-conditioned charter bus then takes care of transporting the refugees to Cairo. Many of those who leave Gaza stay in Egypt, waiting for the end of the war. Or else they go to Turkey or United Arab Emirates, the only countries that readily issue visas to us Palestinians. Malaysia, the only country where we can stay without a visa, would technically be a possibility. But it's too expensive to live there.

After so much rain, suddenly the sun returns. Conditions become calmer, but only because there hasn't been any aid coming in for days, so there's no reason for us to be at each other's throats. The news arriving from Israel, however, worries us. Benny Gantz, a leader of the opposition who agreed to join the war cabinet, repeats that Rafah will be attacked if Hamas doesn't release the hostages before the beginning of Ramadan on March 10. This scenario is disturbing, not just for us in Gaza, but for the whole Palestinian Muslim community—in the West Bank, in East Jerusalem, and in Arab Israeli cities. The holy month is a time for unity and family, of fasting and shared dinners, a moment of peace.

The war by now has destroyed our prayer rituals. Religious sites were the first to be targeted. The few mosques still standing are almost always closed. The only exception is in Rafah's Al-Salam neighborhood, because the mosque there is famously independent, not aligned with any political faction. The faithful go there in the early morning hours; it is, however, a risky place to be. Most believers pray at home or in a tent. The impossibility of properly addressing yourself to your God, however, simply increases the general level of anger. And now Israel announces that it will also limit access to the Al-Aqsa Mosque during the holy month. I speak on the phone about this with friends in the West Bank and Jerusalem, and they're all furious. At this point, they see it as a "religious war" waged by a government half-full of fanatical extremists who violate the freedom of religion.

New leaflets fall on our heads, asking, "Do you want a better future for your family?" They're searching for informants; the army wants to get tips about the hostages. There are numbers to call, with the guarantee that anyone giving information will have their identity protected.

We hear Biden ask Netanyahu not to invade Rafah, but we no longer put our faith in the Americans. The ground invasion will begin soon; negotiations seem to have reached a stalemate.

For now, anyone who has an Egyptian passport can go out. With no warning, our friend Fatma, the scrappy lawyer, decides to leave along with her sister. We're shocked. Their absence sends our small community into crisis. We cry at their departure, hugging them, but we're also happy for them. Fatma's departure makes up my mind as well. The crowdfunding set up for my daughters has succeeded beyond any expectations. I have enough money to send them across. So I file an application on the Hala Agency website and wait. If everything goes as planned, by the end of March they'll be in Egypt. In Cairo, they'll ask for student visas and transfer to Amsterdam, in the Netherlands, where they hope to be able to continue their studies. Except for Bisan's sad trips to Tel Aviv for her treatments at the hospital and an excursion to the Jordan River valley, they've only ever been in Gaza. None of us have ever been in Europe. Egypt will be their door to the world.

## The Dream of a Truce

**In Gaza City, in Jabalia,** in what remains of Beit Lahia, and in the other northern villages, there is no more food to be found. I speak with my sister Samya every chance I get. And I hear from her about the desperate conditions of the 250,000 people still in that part of Gaza. After days in which all phone connections with the North went dead, we finally manage to speak. She's still in my home, together with her husband, children, and grandchildren. They're drinking polluted water, with severe effects on their health. They have nothing except canned beans, and they eat only every other day because their supplies are running out. Their desperation is such that they're sending their oldest boy out to search for leftover food in the rubble of destroyed houses. In fact, my nephew did find a small sack of rice in what was left of a bombed-out home; for the family, it was an occasion to celebrate. Still, despite everything, they feel fortunate. My sister knows at least six children who have died from hunger. The depth of desperation leads to certain spontaneous outbursts. In Jabalia, crowds march in the streets, shouting, "We're starving to death! Enough Hamas already!"

Egyptian sources are again discussing possible truces, and we'll grasp at anything just to regain some peace of mind. They say that Hamas is willing to release the hostages in exchange for 3,000 Palestinian prisoners and a forty-five-day halt to the bombing. We again hope to spend the month of Ramadan in safety; it won't be a return to normalcy, but, during the holy month, at least we won't be afraid. We need to believe it might happen; too often, agreements are said to be close, then they vanish.

In Paris, they're holding talks that make us anxious with optimism. We hear the word "ceasefire" repeated everywhere. We also discuss at length the plan that Netanyahu has presented to his cabinet for postwar Gaza. It envisions no role for UNRWA, the main organization for aid distribution, and it plans buffer zones that would swallow up the areas of northern Gaza. They also speak about installing "local officials with administrative experience who are not tied to countries or entities that support terrorism." It's not said who these officials would be or who would choose them. To me, it seems increasingly clear that Israel wants at least half of the Strip for itself.

Such a prospect is horrible; it brings back the dark times when there were settlers in Gaza. I remember it well. They took possession of the best land; they controlled the water supply. Their presence made development difficult; commercial activity and new construction were suspended. All that mattered was their security. The most modern and beautiful part of Gaza City—now destroyed—sprang up after they left. On the other hand, back then it was at least possible to make a living by working in Israel, since the border was open. Today that's unthinkable. Everyone here says the same thing: "We don't want Hamas, but we also don't want new settlers. They would be hostile and dangerous." What would come with them, we're certain, is some form of apartheid. We already have a Palestinian Authority. We want to choose new leadership from our own people. We want elections.

## *Farewell Party*

The departure of Fatma marks the dissolution of our group. Almost everyone, fearing the imminent invasion of Rafah, moves to our tent city, which is now ready. The girls and I stay in the city; they'll be leaving soon, and their Egyptian visa and journey to Cairo are already paid for. We're just waiting for their names to appear on the Hala Agency's lists. We can't risk moving to that area, where there's no phone or internet; we wouldn't be able to check the lists in time.

Yet I would also like them to leave Gaza, the land where they were born, with memories better than those from these last months of war. So I use up my savings and organize a picnic for them with friends and relatives, at the tent site, where all the others are now living. I manage to score a small piece of lamb from a butcher who lately has had only chicken. Apparently, if you pay enough, you can get it sent in frozen. We roast it outside and offer our friends the chance to eat something they haven't tasted for the last five months. A friend builds us a small outdoor oven from mud and clay; we cook our bread in it as well. It's the same type of oven that our grandmothers used to cook with, except that in those days they were much bigger; these days a lot of people have learned how to make miniature versions. The day is sunny, and we're in front of the sea. It would almost be beautiful if we hadn't heard the distant echo of bombing five times, a reminder of how horribly close the war still is. Nonetheless, our meal is quite cheerful, enlivened by the stories we tell about former times, people and places now gone, and parties we attended, which today seem as magical as fairy tales. Everyone hugs Ruba and Bisan again and again, and the girls seem cheered up at last by this afternoon of "peace."

As we're eating, we see airplanes with no insignias coming toward us. For a moment we fear the worst: an attack by paratroopers, the beginning of a new type of invasion. And in fact parachutes do open. Falling from the sky are crates full of provisions that Jordan has decided to deliver to the area most crowded with refugees, west of Khan Yunis. Inside each crate are dozens of small black bags. Each contains a complete meal for one person, divided into three dishes, similar to military rations: bread and cheese, chicken and rice, a dessert. There is even pain medication.

Whoever manages to get one of these will really have a picnic. But from the very start, getting ahold of them is anything but easy. Dozens of people rush toward each of the crates. There are shouting matches, pushing and shoving, and worse. For now, it's the only option. Egypt and Jordan have tried to negotiate with the Israeli army, hoping to make it possible for Palestinian police to return to the streets and protect arriving aid convoys. But neither the police nor Israel have agreed. And so, to feed the most desperate, food is now literally raining from the heavens. Only the youngest and strongest, able to jostle their way into the throng that the deliveries provoke, succeed in getting hold of a bag. They get food, but it's only one meal. It won't be enough.

At the end of the day, I ask for a photo to be taken of me with my daughters—the last of us together for who knows how long. The picture is taken at sunset, and the girls look really beautiful.

## *The Flour Massacre*

**In Gaza City, during the night** between February 28 and 29, at 4:00 AM, yet another predictable atrocity is committed. The Israeli army opens fire on a hungry crowd that has been waiting for hours for some trucks—roughly thirty, loaded with flour—headed for the neighborhood of Rimal, among the few supply convoys allowed into the North. It happens in a split second in the Nabulsi traffic circle, near Al Rashid Street. According to the army's official version, the crowd tried to storm the convoy and ended up crushed by trucks in the chaos. But eyewitness speak about soldiers who shot deliberately at the thousands of civilians gathered there. And then, the soldiers wouldn't allow the ambulances to approach; they forced the victims to be transported to the hospital by donkey carts brought there for loads of flour. One hundred and sixteen die, and seven hundred more are wounded.

The declaration of the Israeli soldiers attributing the large numbers of dead to the crush of the crowd is contradicted by medical testimony: "The majority of the wounded display lesions caused by gunshots and artillery; the story that the civilians were crushed by trucks is false," states Jadallah al-Shafei, the director of nursing at Al-Shifa Hospital, speaking to Al Jazeera.

The tension, in any case, is present everywhere. Three days earlier, a member of the Kafarne family—he and his family just arrived in Rafah from Beit Hanoun—was wounded by a Palestinian police officer after he, along with others, had been following an aid truck, presumably to rob it. A few hours later, his sons get revenge by killing the officer.

***Volunteers bringing dead bodies to the hospital on donkey carts.***

# MARCH

## *A Lost Generation*

**The flour massacre provokes another** halt to aid distribution in the North, where people continue to die of hunger, as my sister Samya confirms. Now that they've finished off the last of their stockpile, she tells me, they've started to eat grass. At times they make the older children risk the six-hour walk from the far North to Gaza City and back with a sack of flour bought on the black market. Israel wants to finish us off this way too: starving us, halting aid with arbitrary excuses and constantly changing rules.

They have even begun to accuse UNRWA—the last agency with the capacity to help us—to render our survival even more difficult. Whatever the Americans, Egyptian, and Jordanians toss from the sky matters little. You have to be lucky, young, strong, and even cruel to get hold of those food packets. Even if one of those crates does happen to fall on your head, it no longer matters; you still have to defend it from a starving mob ready to flatten you. I wouldn't know how to do it, and I don't even try.

The aid drops also cause people to risk drowning in the sea. The wind pushes many of the crates dropped by parachute into the water. And getting them is dangerous, since the army doesn't allow either fishermen or regular people to venture out in their boats. Nonetheless, to get hold of one of those crates, people crowd onto makeshift rafts. But if they do manage to retrieve something without getting shot at, these desperate souls still find a menacing crowd waiting for them on shore, more desperate and starving than they are, ready to take the longed-for meals away from them. This too is part of the Israeli war strategy: they want to show the world that we Palestinians are savage barbarians, ready to kill our own for food.

I also speak with my cousin, a respected dentist. He stayed in the North because his wife is gravely ill with lung disease, from smoking plus everything she's been breathing in from the bombing. For five days they've eaten only grass, and it's made them sick. He confirmed that the aid drops are happening there as well, but that around every crate, it's complete chaos. He tells me, "We'll die from starvation because I'm not savage enough to beat up other people who are as hungry as me."

It's predictable. Anger is quickly channeled toward wholesalers and storeowners who may be exploiting this extreme situation; they might, for example, take goods off the shelves for a time, only to later triple the price, with the effect of turning basic necessities into luxury goods. Now a couple of pounds of sugar costs twenty dollars, and a packet of cigarettes costs sixty. I usually smoke a ton, but now I have to be happy with buying a single cigarette from time to time, paying five bucks a pop. It doesn't surprise me, then, to see the placards in the town square saying, "Sinwar, Haniyeh, we want to eat with dignity."

To deal with the disappearance of police, some people are trying to organize; a group of volunteers calling themselves "Free Men of Rafah" puts some patrols in place. They also give the shop owners an ultimatum: if prices aren't lowered within a week, they will be punished and their goods confiscated.

It is increasingly evident that the war has created new forms of social hierarchy determined by an individual's specific level of desperation. It doesn't matter who, in our previous lives, were teachers, doctors, or farmers. Whoever doesn't have work, or friends abroad ready to send money and phone cards, falls into the lower strata of society. And there their true nature emerges. The weakest humiliate themselves by begging; the cruelest demand bribes for permission to travel a few yards down a road. Still others become jackals, capable of stealing shoes from the dead or rummaging through the rubble of houses to find loot for resale on the black market.

I see tiny children pleading for the skin of an onion or a sip of clean water. And youths capable of threatening men five times their age. Such social brutalization is very sad. The sons and daughters of Gaza are becoming a lost generation.

## Ramadan

**Everywhere people are debating how** to celebrate the holy month. I'm not religious, but Ramadan is still a holiday I love, something our family has always celebrated. Sharing a meal after long hours of fasting is a moment of serenity, deeply rooted in our culture. We're discussing how we'll manage to observe its precepts in such dramatic conditions. For months, in effect, we've been subjected to a compulsory Ramadan; we have only one meal a day (which puts us among the fortunate), but because we're forced to, not because we're celebrating anything.

Some are saying that the situation in Gaza falls under the exceptions permitted to the sick and to pregnant women; when someone is dying from hardship, they shouldn't renounce whatever sustenance they may receive from dawn to dusk. And fasting is possible only when, at the end of the day, you have enough to eat your fill. But meat and vegetables, the main dishes of a typical evening meal, are either costly or unavailable. It's also impossible to observe the holiday's social traditions: visiting friends and family. Generally, the religious authorities issue edicts to follow in extraordinary circumstances, anticipating the necessary exceptions. This time, however, no one says anything—not Gaza's minister of religion and not the local imams. If these leaders aren't dead, they've clearly taken off their robes. Nothing even from the religious authorities in neighboring countries. We feel abandoned just when we have most need of God.

I patrol Rafah looking for some glimpse of the traditional colored lights in the form of a crescent moon; usually we put them up outside our windows, starting in the days just before Ramadan begins. Only the PalTel telephone company has done something; near the market, the company has set up two tents with lights and games for children, an attempt to boost their morale a bit. In recent months, PalTel has helped us enormously, giving out free minutes for phone calls and offering free network connections whenever possible, even if the signal is often too weak. No one else seems to have enough energy to mark the beginning of our holy month. The faithful say that they'll do their best regardless. Others can't decide—they're too weak and hungry to give up the little food they have.

It's absurd how this war places such profound decisions before us, even from a spiritual perspective. The NGOs responsible for aid distribution report that, for some time now, only enough food to sustain 10 percent of the population has been coming into the Strip. To me, it's obvious even without the numbers. I look at friends I meet in the street, and I see how they've lost weight; their faces have hollowed out, their bodies look weaker. Clothes that we've been wearing for months are worn out, and they hang so loosely we look like scarecrows. We're so misshapen by weight loss that sometimes when we meet, we don't even recognize each other. We're ashamed of our bodies. I, for one, in just the last month, lost over fifteen pounds.

Even so, we still manage to joke around. Usually, before Ramadan, everyone asks each other, "Are you going to fast?" This year, the answer is, "I'm already fasting, can't you see how pious I am?" It's the first time we hear friends say that they're waiting for Ramadan to eat, not to fast; we're hoping that there will be a truce and a massive shipment of aid. Healthy food, not the stuff we usually find that's already past its sell-by date, a victim of long waits at the border. And fresh food— we desperately need fresh vegetables.

The closer the date gets, the more it becomes clear that there will be no truce. Eventually, Hamas tells us, with no half-measures, that it has rejected the Israeli proposals. Some people see this as an attempt to add pressure to the negotiations, but I'm no longer optimistic.

It's not the first wartime Ramadan I've faced. It happened already in 2014, but then we were in our own homes, and in that conflict, the dead were "just" 2,000. At the time, that number seemed enormous, but it was nothing compared to now, with nearly 30,000.

Usually, during the night that heralds the beginning of the holy month, families get together at 3:00 AM to share a light meal. During this period our workday is also lighter; it gets shortened from eight to six hours. We gather again at sunset to eat and drink together. Our single daily meal usually begins with vegetable soup, which serves the important function of reintroducing energy and liquids into the body after it was deprived of them for so many hours. A very sweet fruit juice is served as well, to reintegrate the body's sugar levels. Now there is neither fruit nor vegetables to be had. And even if they were available, our kitchens aren't capable of preparing these foods, and without electricity, we don't have refrigerators to store them.

I close my eyes and think back to the times when our family would come together, go to the mosque to pray, and then be off to cafés and restaurants, staying at the beach for the entire night. The ruckus would continue till dawn, when, with the first prayer, another day of fasting would begin.

I really miss the qatayef, a sort of raviolo stuffed with cream, hazelnuts, and walnuts, traditionally sold by street vendors. Its fragrance is universally recognized as typical of Ramadan, because it's made only at that time of the year. A baker in Rafah tells me that now it's impossible to make it because there's not enough sugar.

The first day goes by "peacefully": there's bombing only in the morning. The only sign that Ramadan has arrived are the women up at dawn, searching nonetheless to scrape together as much food as possible for their loved ones. For those that they have around them, since this year families continue to stay separated. Including mine. In the Rafah markets, there is a bit more than usual, a sign that sellers have been storing goods for the occasion. There are no sweets, dried fruit, and fresh vegetables, however.

In spite of everything said during recent days, almost everyone is still fasting. In situations like this, people become more religious.

They seek the power of God. Even non-practitioners, who are generally less rule-bound, tell me they're observing the precepts. They say, "We're fasting anyway, so why not do it for a reason?" I'm fasting too—as a form of cultural resistance.

# *Nights in a Tent*

**Aid continues to rain down** from the heavens, dropped also in the South by planes from the US, France, Egypt, and Jordan. But it's not enough to keep many people from starving to death; in fact, air transport carries much less aid than the trucks. Letting the trucks across the border would be simpler and more useful.

I speak by phone for a long time to my sister Samya. She tells me that, in the North, the first six aid trucks have come in from Israel. A good sign, but nothing so far has gotten to them. They're still starving. The UNRWA distribution network has been destroyed, so the Israelis have tried contacting local clan leaders to get them to take it on. Only the Dugmush family accepted. Mafiosi by reputation, they're a family of criminals and scoundrels. They had barely begun the work when their leader was assassinated by Hamas, as a "collaborator." No one will mourn him. Although competitors, the Dugmush and Hamas are indistinguishable. They were both holding back basic necessities from the poor so that prices would increase. Like the mafia.

Life in Rafah is getting more dangerous all the time. My daughters have gotten their student visas for the Netherlands, but, so far, their names haven't appeared on the list for leaving Gaza. And so I decide to spend at least a few days with them in the tent city on the beach, where our other friends are staying. That way, we'll also be closer to my mother and to theirs. And we'll be able to visit them more easily during Ramadan.

The organization there is perfect. Each family has their own tent, and there's one larger, central tent used as the kitchen. We meet there to drink tea—with no sugar, because it's already gone. The kitchen is a common space, and basic necessities are shared. Each family also has its own stock of food. We all eat together, though, and share what we have. The clay oven for bread-baking is still working. But it takes a lot of wood to feed it, so we also use the oven for heat, not just for cooking.

Before we arrived, there had already been a small bathroom on the site. There's a toilet for the needs of the farm workers as well as a small shower—cold water, of course. We built a second in a tent nearby, connecting to the same plumbing. Two bathrooms, though, aren't sufficient for sixty people. We add a third. It's not hard to build, but obtaining the necessary materials is unbelievably more expensive this time: we spend almost $500. It's a serious problem, one of many in this small community where everyone has different needs and desires. There are also two elders who aren't able to take care of themselves; they spend a long time in the bathroom, and someone has to take them there and bring them back out. The children are happy, though; after months of being shut in, now they've been let loose to play outside.

The joy of the morning has already turned into a nightmare by nightfall. The girls and I sleep in our clothes, with layers and layers on. Even under the blankets, we suffer from the terrible cold, and we keep waking up. The tents, moreover, are made of wood and nylon: hot as hell in the day, freezing at night. We're also kept awake by the din of bombing in an area called Hamad, built with the help of Qatar years ago, when housing was given to the most desperate in the Strip. I realize that here the war is much closer. I continue to believe, however, that I'm in a secure area. We're in farmland with no buildings, a place where the army has repeatedly sent the residents of Khan Yunis during evacuations.

By morning, though, I've decided: I'll go back and forth with Ruba and Bisan each day from Rafah. We need to have an internet connection to know when their names appear on the list. In the tent city, where there's no signal, I need to leave regularly in order to check.

Plus, although there is a stock of food, it's only enough for a few weeks. We put it together, convinced that a truce will be signed before the beginning of Ramadan, and we'll be able to buy more then. Instead, there's a real risk that the conflict will continue, and that we'll have to make do with the amount we've already put aside.

I return to Rafah with the girls, even though I no longer feel safe in the city. On the news, the talk is about escalation. The bombardments intensify, and the rumble of the bombs keeps getting closer. An attack kills seventeen people very close to where we are. Yet another reason for stress. I need to make decisions quickly, and I can't afford to be wrong. I need to calculate risks, evaluate consequences, and constantly study the situation. I know that sooner or later, Ruba and Bisan will be called and allowed to leave, but when I pester them on the phone, the agency tells me that the demand is now so high that wait times have increased by two more weeks. I start to be afraid—whoever doesn't get out before the inevitable invasion of Rafah will no longer be able to leave the Strip.

## *Ruba and Bisan Leave*

**Just when I'm about to lose all hope**, the news we've expected for twenty-two days arrives. My daughters, Ruba and Bisan, can leave Gaza. I'm very worried about them; they've never traveled alone. And I don't know if or when I'll see them again. My heart is in turmoil. Still, in a few hours, they'll eat a decent meal. They'll have a hot shower. They'll start to live again. Holding on to that, I reconcile myself with the idea of letting them go.

It all happens very fast. And due to an incredible series of events, we even risk missing the crucial meeting.

I had paid the Hala Agency on February 20. I thought they would be leaving in three weeks. But every time I called to remind them, a courteous agent on the other line would tell me, "Their names will be on the list tomorrow, or the day after tomorrow at the latest ..." The dizzying increase in exit requests had slowed everything down.

I didn't say anything to the girls, because I didn't want to demoralize them, but I had almost given up hope. So much so that I brought them to sleep in the tent city so they would start adapting to that way of life. However, I also realized that staying in the area meant that we risked missing the chance to get them out. It was too difficult to get online and check the list of names when they were posted, around 10:00 PM. I had to go over a half mile by foot in the dark of night. So I accepted the risk of bringing them back to Rafah, though I was ready to turn back at the first sign of an invasion.

Sometimes the list of approved names is posted late, in the middle of the night. When it finally happens, after so many disappointments, I'm not expecting it. Exhausted, I'd gone to bed at 10:30 PM. At midnight, I wake up at the beep from a message. Then I get another. I don't have the energy to open my eyes. But the messages keep coming. Finally, I wake up completely, and I read them. It takes me a minute to comprehend. Friends and relatives have just seen the list online—it's most closely followed newsletter in Gaza—and they're offering congratulations for the girls' imminent department and wishing them good luck. It's very late but I wake them up. We don't sleep for even a minute more.

Everything is ready, but even so I always feel like something is missing. We unpack and repack the suitcases two times. We check the official documents, addresses, telephone numbers, computers, and battery chargers. We start calling people—yes, at that hour—to say goodbye. They say goodbye to their grandmother. They call their mother, still sheltering in Khan Yunis. And they also speak with their cousins, who we left behind up north, since they're very close. By dawn, they're no longer willing to listen to reason at all; they run everywhere to hug their best friends, waking up their entire families.

We have a last breakfast together: bread and tea with no sugar. They have no appetite at all, but I force them to get a few bites down. They have a long day in front of them, and they won't be able to manage it on an empty stomach. At 8:30, I go with them to the gates at the border, which ought to be opening at 9:00. And then I almost die from a heart attack—I find out that, because of the number of people, the official opening is now at 8:00. So we're a half hour late! Luckily, the line is moving very slowly, and there are still a lot of people outside. We hug. We cry. We say goodbye to each other. Finally, they go in. I keep my eyes glued on my phone, so I can follow every step they take. I have already pleaded with them, "Write to me about everything. I want to be told about every stamp you get on your papers." Luckily, in the crowd getting ready to leave, they find an old friend of mine. He writes to me immediately, telling me that he's taken them under his wing. I couldn't hope for anything better.

It takes them three hours just to cross the Palestinian border. In that area, cell phones don't work. After not hearing from them for such a long time, I start to imagine crazy things: they've been arrested, or kidnapped ... Instead, they reappear once they're on the Egyptian side of the border. But to get through still takes them three more hours. And their documents do in fact get inspected in minute detail. Their passports, like those of many people in Gaza, had expired. We had to have them renewed in Ramallah by proxy. From there, they were sent to Egypt, because there was no way to have them sent back to us; the postal service has been destroyed like everything else. Luckily, the Egyptian authorities are aware of all this. It's become a normal procedure, even though it's expensive; a Hala employee brings the documents to the border and delivers them to their waiting customers. It's called "VIP treatment." Given what it costs, that's the least they could do.

Finally, the girls tell me that they've gotten over the border. It's 4:00 in the afternoon. They get on the bus waiting for them, and in their assigned seats they find something that here in Gaza we can only dream about: water and a snack. (During Ramadan, travelers are permitted to eat.) The journey across the Sinai will last six hours.

They call me, overcome with emotion, before they get on the bus. And then three more times. They send me a selfie from a cafeteria where they stop for a half-hour break. There are thirty other people traveling with them. They send me photos of small children, taken as they drive through a village; they're amazed that, just a few miles away from the hell of Gaza, life continues. I try to rest, but I'm too anxious; it's impossible for me to sleep. By the time they get to Cairo, it is already night, but since it's Ramadan, the city is full of lights and life. One of my cousins is waiting for them. At his house, they find a table full of delicacies. His family can't stop hugging them and giving them more food than they can eat.

The next morning, they sleep late. It's the first time in five months that they sleep in a clean bed, take a hot shower, and put on freshly washed clothes. I'm in a daze—euphoric and desperate at the same time. I can't manage to concentrate on anything, and I send them messages nonstop.

I feel exhausted. Emptied out. I do have to get back to my job, though; I have a duty to tell the dramatic story of my people in Gaza. Thanks to the help of many, I managed to get my daughters to safety. But it pains me to know that no one worries about saving so many other girls and boys, so many children just like them.

Despite these reservations, friends that I meet hug me and shake my hand, wishing me good luck and blessings—as if, instead of getting out of a war zone, my daughters had just graduated or gotten married, as if they'd reached some major goal in life. Because in this place, life is suspended. Whoever manages to get out is celebrated as a star.

## *Friends*

**My daughters call me just** after they wake up. They tell me that they went to bed exhausted and stuffed with food—something that hadn't happened since the war began—and that they slept like never before. My friend Fatma, who is also in Cairo, comes to get them for a tour of the city. They send me a selfie, and in the photo I see three free women. It's the first time that my girls take on a challenge like this, yet there they are, smiling and happy. They're more courageous than me.

Me, on the other hand, I'm wiped out. But my mix of joy and melancholy keeps me flying like a kite, and I can't manage to sleep. My beautiful daughters are now safe in Cairo, although their journey was really long, and I was terrified the whole time. Trying to protect them was my main worry over these last months, and now I feel empty. I'm alone, in a world on fire, where every last shred of humanity is vanishing. Now that they're safe, I struggle to think that until yesterday they were here, at risk like me, bent on surviving, as if war had always been a part of our lives. I had almost forgotten that there was a world outside.

My friends from the tent city call me, reporting that—just a few hundred yards from that place we considered the safest spot in the Strip—there has been bombing and people were killed. It was horrible. My friends had to flee to the beach, with babies wailing in their arms, and for six hours they stayed there, their feet in the water, because they were too afraid to go back to their shelter. They were scared to death; some of them are already saying it was a mistake to create something that looks like a village. It could attract the military's attention, and perhaps it would be safer to go back to Rafah. They believe this in part because, according to rumors, there won't be a large-scale invasion before the end of Ramadan. The hypocrisy of war: the Israelis might not want to cause a massacre during the holy month, as if killing or dying in some other moment somehow counts less, or more. In my state of exhaustion or agitation, I have trouble imagining what it would have been like in the tent city with Ruba and Bisan in that moment of horror. How could I have endured yet again my daughters sobbing from fear? I simply couldn't have born the anxiety of having them one day more here in Gaza. But at the same time, I don't know how I'll manage to bear not having them here. I'm consoled again by the thought that they'll be going back to school.

It's the first Friday of Ramadan. My mother wants to have more of her children with her, even though she already has my brother Ahmed and my second sister, Siham, who has fled from Gaza City with her son and daughter. Hassan and I decide to go, knowing how important the Ramadan meal is for her. She's making maqluba for us, a typical holiday dish, and so easy to make that it's considered perfect for people who don't like to cook. Maqlubeh in Arabic means "upside down," which is the main feature of the dish. You cook it by putting the ingredients in the pan in layers: first meat, if there is any, then rice and vegetables. Then, before bringing it to the table, you turn it upside down—a difficult maneuver, and one that doesn't always work, but it always tastes good anyway.

During dinner, my mother peppers me with questions about how the war is going. She repeats one question in particular: "When will we go home?" I answer, "Soon." But we both know that it's just for show. She lists for me everything that she misses: first, her bed, more than anything else. She keeps hitting her palm on her forehead, "How could I have forgotten ..." She names every single object, things that have no value, except for her. Her memories.

The next day I don't go back to Rafah; there's no one waiting for me there anymore. Instead, I head to the tent city where my friends are. We share our Ramadan meal together, making an effort to maintain our dignity. We set up a single, long table outside, and everyone brings something to share. And we somehow succeed, unbelievably, to create a festive atmosphere. Constantly, though, the shooting in the distance and the buzzing of drones overhead bring us back to reality. In an extraordinary effort to return to the ordinary, the women have managed to prepare a traditional dish, qatayef. Most of the ingredients are missing, and it doesn't taste right, but we eat it anyway.

The tent city is well organized, but it's still far from the city. For now, the three of us who commute for work to Rafah or Khan Yunis do the shopping for the rest as well. Spending our evenings among people we know and trust reassures us. But we are afraid there may be militants hidden in nearby tents, so Israeli's bombardments might also hit here. In the distance we do see soldiers and tanks; we hear shooting. Fear is constant. We hope that Israeli operations in Khan Yunis will end soon. That beautiful city—its buildings funded by many different Arab countries—has by now been totally destroyed. We're afraid it's a sign of what will happen to Rafah.

Despite so much devastation, I think something still exists that no one has managed to destroy, something that in fact grows stronger: the friendship within our group. We're constantly in contact with each other. And strong new bonds have been born. If, on one hand, we're experiencing extreme brutality, on the other, solidarity and openness persist. Such values are indispensable to the survival of a society pushed to the breaking point, where most people think only of themselves and outside help is lacking. I feel grateful to the extraordinary people who have taken me in, first in Khan Yunis and then in Rafah. I've met exceptional families, capable of brightening dark days with their smiles and sense of humor.

And I also have my friends for life. The closest are Mohammed and Sami, both ex-journalists at WAFA, the Palestinian news agency where I worked in my youth. Like me, they lived in the North and are now in Rafah. Sami lives in a tent in the western part of the city.

*Sami's daughters with members of his chosen family in Khan Yunis. From the left: Taher, Ruba, Besan, Haya, Neven, and little Batoul.*

Mohammed is in a house near the Egyptian border, in the Al-Salam neighborhood. We meet often, and we talk about our lives years ago, before the war, when we dreamed of a better future, one far from here and far from Hamas.

With them, I discuss the UN Security Council resolution calling for an immediate ceasefire in Gaza—approved after an unprecedented abstention from the United States. We welcome it, but without any illusions. From the news services, which we follow attentively, we perceive quite clearly that the international community now views Israel with new eyes. Netanyahu understands this, and it irritates him, but he still believes he can operate outside the law, despite the isolation that has become increasingly evident.

This time we really do hope that Israel won't disappoint us and will accept a ceasefire until the end of Ramadan. Not least because in recent days the bombing by Israel seems, if possible, even more intense. Here in Rafah, four neighborhoods in the city have been hit, causing sixteen deaths and wounding dozens more. Meanwhile, in the middle of the Strip, attacks continue against Nasser and Al-Amal hospitals in Khan Yunis. Civilians and patients are forced to flee, and the medical staff is arrested.

## *Downward Spiral*

**Five of my colleagues kept** working in Gaza City. I used to speak with them every day, since they were the only ones capable of telling us what life was like in that area, cut off from the rest of the world. They continued to do their job, despite suffering from starvation like everyone in the North. And, alas, those five journalists have now been arrested. Among them is Ismail al Ghoul, a reporter for Al Jazeera.

As part of an ongoing military operation inside Al-Shifa Hospital, they were taken with brute force and their equipment destroyed. During this attack, according to Israel, Faiq Mabhuoch, head of internal security operations for Hamas, was killed. No explanations were given for the arrest of the journalists along with some members of the medical staff. I'm afraid for them all. I fear they'll be tortured and end up in very nasty prisons, simply because they were there. The Israelis call journalists "supporters," but my friends were only doing their job. They saw tanks entering the city, and so they went over to the hospital. I would have done the same. During the various wars in Gaza, that's where you get the most information. The wounded arrive there—eyewitnesses to the events. Ismail and the others were working; arresting them demonstrates once again that Israel's real aim is to silence us journalists, so that no one reports on the horrors of all that is happening here.

Our profession is becoming more and more difficult. Our lives are constantly in danger; we're liable to be arrested and tortured by the Israelis, but we're also unwelcome among our own citizens, who consider us potential targets. Being seen at our side is risky, and even our families have been singled out and ostracized by our community. No one is willing to tell us their stories anymore; they're too frightened they will be exposed as a witness. For this reason, fewer and fewer of us are left to describe what is happening in Gaza. It's dangerous; those who aren't arrested are killed. I already have 130 dead colleagues.

On the rotunda at Kuwait Square in Gaza City, where aid is distributed and where just a few days ago there was a massacre, another twenty-three people are killed in yet another raid. The majority are volunteer members of the self-organized "people's committees" that provide security during the aid distribution. The official target, according to the army, was the group's leader, Amjad Abhat, said to have ties to the militants. Those who died, however, were civilians not involved with the militants. To avoid a massacre, this attack could have been done with precision weapons. Instead, these sorts of operations seem to intentionally aim at disrupting aid distribution and further starving the population. In Israeli's eyes, we're all guilty; the people's committees are tied to Hamas, they say. They make the same argument about UNRWA or any other NGO that tries to help us. Who then ought to distribute the food? Sure, many men who are ready and willing to work security used to be employed by the government. But today they are the only people capable of ensuring the orderly distribution of aid—at least until a new government is established or imposed. We need security.

In the meantime, Israeli jets fly by at very high speed and very close to the ground, breaking the sound barrier. They do it simply to frighten us even more with their deafening noise. Our terror now combines with a new form of pessimism: we have become afraid that Israel will attack before the end of Ramadan. "Without destroying Rafah, there can be no victory," says Netanyahu. The offensive may occur in a matter of days. On the street, people are saying that the leaders of Hamas have already left Gaza with their families. One example, Ismail Haniyeh, is known to be safely abroad already, for some time now. Now the second-rank officials are fleeing too, like the spokesperson for the Minister of Health, Ashraf al-Qudra, and the spokesperson for the police, Iman Batanji. In the street, many people are saying that, "after having provoked the war and having permitted the destruction of our land, they are abandoning us, leaving us alone to face the consequences of their actions."

The Americans have begun to construct a pier to help bring in more aid. They say it will be temporary, but they're using the rubble from buildings flattened by the bombing. We're skeptical. There are already ways to access Gaza. All it would take is a willingness to allow in the cargo of the hundreds of trucks blocked just on the other side of the Rafah crossing. We fear that the pier may become yet another system used to chase us Palestinians out of the Strip. Not now, but soon. Maybe after they've dehumanized us to the point where—after a life in tents on a beach—all we want is to leave.

## *Same Pain, Same Hunger*

**The third Friday of Ramadan** is also Good Friday for the few Christians left here, as they prepare to celebrate Easter. We are all suffering together, regardless of faith. We are living through the same pain, the same destruction, the same hunger, and therefore we all support each other. In Gaza City, at the small Holy Family Church, which was already severely damaged in Israeli attacks, the Catholics are beginning Easter services. They have welcomed in the Orthodox Christians who had first taken refuge in the Church of Saint Porphyrius, destroyed months ago now. And some Muslim families are also harbored within these same bounds. All receive food and shelter. They pray together—Catholics, Orthodox Christians, and Muslims.

With my brother Hassan, I go to visit my mother, as I did on the other Fridays during Ramadan. On the way there, we encounter a large group of people gathered around an imam who is presiding over a religious rite, with the help of a megaphone. Seeing such a scene, which was once normal, astonishes me. Since the start of the war, I haven't witnessed anything like it. Like everyone here, I'm exhausted.

We live under a condition of constant stress. We eat poorly, we can't wash, and we know nothing about our future. Our joy regarding the UN ceasefire resolution quickly gives way to dejection. Israel continues to drop bombs, and the international community fails to exert enough pressure to make it stop. As always, we civilians, including women and children, are the ones who suffer under Israel's wrath—in this instance, anger in response to the American abstention, which allowed the UN measure to pass.

This time, it is the Hasiras, a notable family in Gaza City, who pay the price. Owners of a small fleet of fishing boats and a number of seafood restaurants, they were well known in the local commercial and business sector. They were living close to Al-Shifa Hospital, and a bomb that struck their home killed all thirty members of their clan.

Another eighteen people suffer even more absurd deaths, caused by the aid drops: twelve drown while trying to retrieve food packets that fall into the sea, and six others are killed in clashes over aid they've commandeered. No one I know ever goes near those crates of aid—it's too dangerous. Only the most desperate people turned savage by hunger manage to get their hands on them. Or whoever organizes gangs of youths capable of anything—in a word, criminals.

Hamas calls the aid drops "useless and violent." But we're fed up with statements coming from people who are safely abroad or well protected down in tunnels. They continue to say that Israel is losing the war. Certainly we civilians aren't winning.

## *Rimal No Longer Exists*

**After two weeks of bombing** and raids, the Israeli army leaves Al-Shifa Hospital. The images we get from there show total devastation. I'm in pain, not only for the hundreds of victims, but also because it effectively marks the end of an era of hope and growth. The Rimal quarter, in the heart of Gaza City where the hospital stood, was an elegant neighborhood. Along with the hospital, there was a famous shopping mall that was always crowded. Also an Italian restaurant, the best in the Strip, or so they say. It was my girls' favorite, and we often used to have their excellent pizzas delivered. And then, right in front of Al-Shifa, there was the most historic hotel in the city: Marna House, a three-story townhouse transformed into a boutique hotel, with a very old tree in front and a very pleasant coffee bar in its garden. I started going there when I was young; my parents would take me. And I've continued to visit it regularly, often bringing foreign journalists there for a drink or to smoke a *shisha*. A locale with a cosmopolitan atmosphere.

In the same area, not far away, I also used to go to a small restaurant, owned by Abu Talal, famous for serving "the best falafel in Gaza." My last visit there was in September, a few days before the start of the war.

When I think about those places, so rich with memories for me and now forever destroyed, I'm heartbroken. And I can imagine the torment felt by people who lived in those beautiful apartment buildings; many were among the wealthiest in Gaza, and now they're forced to survive in the tents of Rafah. Their homes in Rimal have all been destroyed by artillery and fires. That's what happened to my friend Eyal, a lawyer specializing in human rights law and manager of an NGO. He stuck it out in Rafah for months, yearning to return home. But when he saw photos of the destruction of his lovely apartment, he paid to transfer himself and his family to Egypt. He said goodbye to me with tears in his eyes.

"We're going somewhere safe before Rafah is attacked. I have nothing to return to."

Now he's in Cairo, living off savings acquired over his entire career. Soon they'll be used up, and I don't know if he has found another job.

# APRIL

# *Six Months Under the Bombs*

**On April 7, I add it up**: we've now been living under these extreme circumstances for 180 days. Certainly the worst days of my life. My beautiful, marvelous Gaza, a magical city capable of resisting even the fanatical thinking of the Islamists, has been destroyed by Israel. My life and my future have disappeared along with it.

During these months, I've been crushed over and over. I've wept often. The first time was when I decided to leave my home behind. Then again, during the assault on the Al-Quds Hospital, when my brother Hassan was among the thousands of people trapped inside. And then, in shock, in front of my father's remains.

I already know that the whole Strip will be little more than a desert after the war—a land forced into the past, stripped of its media, economy, politics, and culture. It will take at least twenty years of peace to return to how it was before October 7. Perhaps the time for reconstruction and progress will never come at all.

We've been under the bombs for six months; we're rapidly coming to the conclusion that this is no temporary situation—it's our new environment. We've grown so inured that we've begun to find strange new forms of resistance; we learn to enjoy what little we have left. I noticed this with the start of spring, the only pleasant season we have, since it's too cold in winter and too hot in summer. The coast road percolated with more life than I could possibly have imagined. I saw men and women coming back to walk on the beach, often with their feet in the water, like it was in the good old days. You see young couples in love, secret lovers who don't walk side by side but instead go back and forth so they at least pass by each other and get to exchange a glance or even a quick word. If instead the engagements are "official," meaning that their families are in the know, the young pairs walk timidly together, holding hands, sometimes with a parent following closely behind, and often a child. Marriages are even taking place again; for a while, no one was celebrating them, in the belief that the war would soon be over. Most of these ceremonies are for couples who were already engaged but then had to postpone everything; now, in this protracted and extreme situation, they no longer want to wait.

One of my friends even organizes a dinner to announce the engagement of his twenty-seven-year-old son, Mohammed. At the end of October, Mohammed was supposed to have married Maran, who is twenty; everything had already been arranged. They had been together for two years and no longer wanted to wait. Naturally, their exchange of vows didn't take place in the sumptuous hotel where they had earlier paid for a banquet. Instead, they had to settle for a downsized dinner with only parents and siblings representing the two families, though that was still a fairly large number. Unlike normal times, there was no dancing and no cake, because it would have cost too much. Plus, with grief all around us, everyone feels guilty for enjoying themselves.

Getting engaged and getting married doesn't in any way mean things are becoming normal. Intimacy remains impossible, and many couples are living frustrated by the absence of their sexual lives. Unfortunately, we're sharing space with dozens of other people. Often, even newly minted spouses are forced to sleep separately, the men in one part, women in another. Making love is nearly impossible. We even laugh about it, joking that the war will surely cause another demographic decrease in the citizenry of Gaza.

Those who had been loving in secret from a distance now really struggle. Before, these sorts of relationships survived thanks to chat rooms and social media. But now internet access is difficult, and talking online with your sweetheart is nearly impossible. In such circumstances, you lose track of each other. Then you fall desperately in love with someone else, often someone in the tent next to you. So new couples form, and tensions ignite. Some get resolved through shotgun weddings. In other cases, an entire family is forced to move.

Even in these extreme circumstances, however, some clandestine couples do manage to find places for privacy, for at least a second or two. They might, for example, take advantage of the chaos from the bombings. I've heard about shadowy figures slinking out from certain tents. Many friends of mine, though, tell me that they don't even think about having sex. It seems impossible to let yourself go when bombs are falling outside and people continue to die.

There's no lack of ill-timed pregnancies. People are forced to terminate them, just as has always happened. Paying women to perform backroom abortions, though, naturally, such topics are taboo. For years, our social conventions have prohibited any form of affection and physical contact outside of marriage. Even speaking of such things is prohibited. Yet it is clear; like all the other sacrifices, depriving the body does take its toll.

## *Berger's Revenge*

**WITH JOY AND WONDER,** I welcome the news that the Israeli army is retreating from the southern part of the Strip. They say they'll leave behind only a single brigade. At the same time, I'm suspicious. I wonder about the motives behind a decision of this sort. Perhaps it's a reaction to American pressure; the White House has just issued a very critical public statement. With only a few months left before the elections, Biden wants the war to end no matter what. To me, this withdrawal from the South seems like a good sign.

The streets are vacant. Many people take advantage, and I'm one. It's Friday, so I do some shopping at the market and go to visit my mother in Deir al-Balah. On the way there, I take a small detour and stop by Hamad's place, west of Khan Yunis. Before the Israeli occupation, it was an area known for modern design, full of shopping malls and supermarkets. I haven't been back there for months. In the past, I visited it often because a close friend, al-Azha, lived there. Since then, he and his family have taken refuge in New York, with a visa provided by the American NGO that employed him. He asked me to check to see what condition his apartment is in, so that's why I go.

I'm still in shock. Most of the buildings are destroyed; through their burned, skeletal structures, I see how the apartments have been vandalized and gutted. It takes me a while to recognize my friend's home. I suddenly find myself standing in front of it. His apartment lies behind a particularly tall pile of rubble, still usable, but there are no windows or doors left, and the furniture is ruined. The soldiers threw grenades inside, as they often do. They must have been going from house to house searching for militants, because the apartment next door is in a similar state.

At this second home, though, I'm struck by some graffiti sprayed in black paint: "Berger's revenge." I wonder who this Berger is. Maybe an Israeli soldier with some friend or relative who was a victim on October 7. At the same time, however, I wonder who this apartment belongs to. Almost certainly a family that has nothing to do with Hamas.

There are many people around me. They're crying in desperation at the sight of their ruined homes. I see them digging through the rubble with their hands, searching for something that will give them back at least some fragment of their past. They're looking for objects with mainly sentimental value. If there were anything really valuable, thieves—whether Palestinian or Israeli—would already have run off with it.

Here's a contradiction in this merciless war: I meet some families that are happy. They can't believe it, but by some miracle, they stand before their apartments and find them intact. Or nearly so, because every home shows some signs of the invasion. If it's still standing, the apartment was likely used by soldiers as cover for their snipers. Afterwards, before leaving, they loot them. Social media sites are full of soldiers posing for selfies that show all the things they found by rummaging through other people's closets and drawers. I see them dressed up in women's clothes, making obscene gestures. Even though they must've put their hands on everything, for the owners of houses that are still intact, it doesn't matter. They know that, at least for now, there's still a place to come home to.

## *Khan Yunis Apocalypse*

**After I spend yet another** Friday with my mother, I venture out to explore nearby Khan Yunis. The reality exceeds my imagination. I feel as if I'm in a film, and the landscape is apocalyptic. No one has been back in the city for months. And now, "visitors" like me are stunned. There used to be a road there; now it's gone. Over there, a bunch of small houses, the homes of Khan Yunis's middle-class—all destroyed. The square has vanished. The parking ramp was swallowed up. The market burned down. Everywhere is the same: rubble and dust. On the street, you even see some wrecked Israeli tanks; they must have been damaged, then apparently abandoned. In apartments still whole because the army used them, you find trash from meals, books in Hebrew, and markings on outside walls left by snipers, to let their fellow soldiers know they were there. Returning to those homes will be impossible; they're still standing but severely damaged.

Here too I find men scavenging through the ruins of their dwellings, helped by their children. Some of them are wounded; I even see a man grinding forward on a wheelchair. They all have rags wrapped around their faces as masks, so they don't breathe in the dust. They pull out dented pots and pans, alarm clocks, broken dishes. They'll bring these things back to Rafah, to the tents that have become their new homes.

I also see another type of person wandering through the rubble: the jackals. They too are digging in search of valuable objects but don't show emotion when they find something, not the way I see others react. They're well organized—they have motorcycles or donkey carts, piled with sacks full of silverware, pocket radios, and shoes. Tomorrow it will all be on display at the market in Rafah.

Fortunately, there are no dead bodies. Around twenty corpses were abandoned on the roadside, but pious first responders alerted UNRWA, and workers came to take them away.

I meet many children. One of them is named Dima Quwaider. She's twelve years old and rarely speaks. Her young aunts, sisters of her mother, brought her here from Rafah; they tell me the story of how Dima became an orphan. Her mother died right here. Her father, however, was killed two months later during one of the bombardments of Deir al-Balah, where they'd found shelter. She misses her parents terribly. I'm told that she alternates between aggressiveness and bouts of sobbing. She has asked over and over to see her home again; now the aunts could finally satisfy her wish. Dima points to the rooms where they lived, saying, "That was the kitchen. Mom and Dad slept there, and that was my room." She finds some of her mother's clothes and weeps silently. She'll bring everything back to the tent where she lives now, with these women who love her but can't really help her.

On the roof of a half-destroyed house nearby, I find Zakaria. He's a nice-looking boy, nineteen years old, and he too lives in a tent in Rafah. He's desperate and sobs loudly. He'll go back with nothing because, to his great sorrow, his house was burned down and nothing can be saved. He utters words of hate: "Hamas and Israel should both die."

From that same area, a few hours after I was there, the militants launch a rocket. They target the area near the Re'im kibbutz, and alarms are triggered in all the Israeli villages across the border. When news of this action arrives, people are furious.

"You're provoking them again? Enough already!"

In any case, it's difficult to know when there are still militants around. They certainly keep well hidden. They're too afraid of being monitored from the sky by the army's drones, which never lose sight of us.

Faced with so much destruction, my early morning optimism dies out. On the radio, I hear Iranian leaders saying Israel's withdrawal is simply tactical. Netanyahu claims that he already has a date set for a rescheduled Rafah invasion. I'm no longer sure that the war is about to end. After all, the Israeli army already pulled out of Gaza City once, only to return and increase the aggression, besieging the Al-Shifa Hospital until it was utterly destroyed.

## *The Tension Spreads*

**Suddenly attention is focused elsewhere.** A few weeks ago, Israel bombed the Iranian consulate in Damascus, Syria, killing, among others, the leader of the Revolutionary Guards. On the evening of April 13, Teheran responds. To us Gazans, it seems like play-acting, two enemies each showing their muscles, but without wanting to engage in a real war, like the one waged against us. What sort of attack is it where the place and hour of the strike are announced in advance?

The situation may be more dramatic than it seems from Gaza, but in the desperate state we find ourselves in, it just inspires laughter. We've been living for six months under bombardment, and it makes us smile when Israel calls this announced-in-advance Iranian operation an "attack." Those tensions have nothing to do with us. In Gaza, only 10 percent of the population thinks that Iran is an ally and a trustworthy partner. The remaining 90 percent don't expect anything from Tehran, except more problems that add to an already complex situation. But then, of course, some people from here do celebrate online. But they don't do it publicly; in the street, they'd risk getting lynched. Fearless warriors of the keyboard, in fundamentalist garb, they prefer performing for their audiences on X or on Facebook.

In any case, while the news about the Iranian attack is spreading around the world, the refugee population in the center of the Strip has other things to think about. Hundreds of people receive new cell phone messages authored by the Israeli army. An invitation to return to the North. The reaction is hysteria: everyone rushes off. They immediately cross through the passage left open by the soldiers, and they also warn their friends and relatives. Thus, from the South as well, people hurry up the coast road. And, as could have been predicted, it unleashes chaos. The mess is such that, a few hours later, the soldiers close the passage again and begin to shoot at the crowd to make it disperse. Within the mob, a three-year-old child is killed. And it turns out that those who were the first to cross get stuck, due to the critical situation in the North. They can't get back. No one can understand why or on whose orders those messages were sent.

We are simply bewildered. Israel's intentions seem incomprehensible. We can't decide if the conflict is about to escalate into a more aggressive phase, or if the ground invasion is finished, and, though the war will continue, there will only be targeted actions with additional warnings. We do know, however, that no one will do anything for us. Least of all the Arab world. We're alone.

As for the rest, Rafah seems quieter, though the specter of invasion is still frightening. The Strip remains divided in two. In the North, starvation continues. In the South, the measure of improvement is the amount of flour arriving. We get a larger weekly distribution, and this causes prices to stabilize. More canned food can be found as well. Some private citizens have managed to get through some frozen beef and chicken. In smaller quantities, you can even find vegetables. In this atmosphere, some people are even starting up new businesses. And not just temporary activities, stable ventures. The problem is the vast majority of evacuees no longer have money. The banks are closed, the ATMs are empty, and merchants only give you small sums, at very high commissions.

## *Leaving*

**I'M LISTENING TO THE NEWS,** which is always the same. Sporadic bombing is still hitting Rafah, and there are other attacks in the north, targeting Beit Hanoun and Jabalia. The war isn't over, but the mood seems almost tranquil.

And so, for the first time since the beginning of the conflict, I go out with my friends and stay out until 11:00 that evening. I meet with some dear friends. We laugh a lot over our collective suffering. We hug each other, amazed to still be alive. We talk about the past, about our homes, about everything we've lost. We tell stories about our past lives, the bars where we used to hang out together, the streets, the restaurants, mutual friends. All places that no longer exist—except in our stories.

In their company, I make an announcement: I'm getting out. After hesitating for weeks, I've decided. I'm leaving Gaza. I've organized everything in secret, without saying anything to anyone, because I have good reason to believe that I as a journalist have now become a target. It's happened already to many others. All of a sudden, you become a problem for them, and you don't even know why. Many of my colleagues are dead already; others have either gotten out or about to go. I feel I'm in serious danger, so I've decided to exhaust my savings and buy a visa from the Hala Agency. To tell the truth, I've changed my mind about it a thousand times over the past month. Just weeks ago, I was so certain I wanted to stay that I sent my daughters away on their own. I'd hoped that knowing they were safe would help me to do my work here more effectively. And at first, it worked. But the situation didn't improve. There are more calm periods than before, but it's a strange sort of calm. The risk is constant.

I'd hoped for quite a while to avoid leaving, convinced that some solution would be found; perhaps there would be a hostage exchange, and with it, a ceasefire that would lead to peace. Events, however, belied my hopes. As a result, I'm heading out, and it shatters me. I'm leaving behind everything I love.

My friends slap me on the back, trying to console me. They wish me the best, but they're sad. Every person who goes leaves a void that can't be filled in those who remain. We spend the rest of the evening talking about the future. We all have the same dilemma: when everything is over, will we go back to our destroyed homes and try to rebuild? Or will we abandon Gaza forever? In this moment, none of us feels they have the strength to keep moving forward.

We switch to the topic of how much money we'll need to survive outside of Gaza. And how we'll manage to earn anything in a foreign country. We'll need plenty. And we realize that the choice we face is a paradox: staying in this hell or getting out and going to countries where there is no war, but also no work permitting us to live with dignity.

Not far from where I'm living more bombs are falling. They hit Yabna, a refugee camp near Rafah. I don't know who was living in the house that was hit, but eleven people die. And once again, half of them are children. A few hours after I see those small, brutalized bodies, I read my name on the list. I can't say if I feel more torment or joy.

It's already night when I call my mother. I tell her, "It's tomorrow." She understands, cries a bit, and whispers a prayer. We said goodbye days ago. But we'd already said goodbye like that many times before; perhaps she wasn't really prepared.

I leave my car with my brother Hassan, and he, along with my friend Saeed, accompanies me early the next morning to the check-in site. We do our best to cheer each other up, joking around right up to

*Leaving Gaza. Sami (center) with his brother Hassan (right) and his friend Saeed (left).*

the end. We snap a photo to mark the occasion. Nonetheless, when it's time for a last hug, none of us manage to keep from crying.

And so, I now face the same itinerary taken by my daughters just a month ago. I join a long line of desperate people, like me, ready to leave their homeland. We smile through our tears, happy to leave the horror behind us. And we cry, knowing that we may never see our loved ones again.

In a few days, it will be Eid al-Fitr, the celebration at the end of the Ramadan fast. What's next? The Israeli plan to push all of Gaza's inhabitants into tent cities on the beach is moving forward. Ending up there is a sentence to hell. And it will last for ages. Whoever doesn't die under the bombs will die from illness and privation. In going away, I feel tremendous guilt toward those I leave behind. I repeat to myself yet again the arguments that convinced me to leave, that in the chaos of the armed invasion of Rafah, I as a journalist would be in danger. Not to mention caught in a trap. In that sort of environment, getting out would no longer be possible. The risk of being stuck here for months, or even for years, is far too concrete. I simply can't bear the thought of not seeing my daughters for who knows how long. Plus, I'm exhausted. These six months of war, always in the field, always telling stories of atrocities and suffering, have shattered me.

But I won't go too far. I'll stay in Egypt, and I'll stay in contact with the people inside. I'll keep telling their stories.

# *Epilogue*

**Leaving Gaza, I weep.** I chose life, but I abandoned the people I love most. It's a terrible feeling, and it doesn't leave me in the days that follow.

At first, I'm too confused by it all to think. I'm happy taking a hot shower any time I feel like it. After so much time in houses packed with people, I rent an apartment far away from the chaos of Cairo. I live by myself.

Solitude helps me comprehend the immense toll of my suffering. Far away from the horrible buzzing of drones, from the rumble of planes, from the din of the bombing, no longer forced to see horrible images, dead bodies in the street and houses destroyed everywhere, I understand how horribly traumatized I am and how my pain is beyond healing.

I sleep little and am shaken by my dreams. I meet almost no one. I stay shut up in my new home, thinking at each moment of my daughters and of the people of Gaza—my family, my friends, my colleagues. I think back through every moment of my life, so suddenly turned upside down.

During the long months of war in Gaza, I refused to listen to my thoughts, to my emotions. I was too busy surviving and taking care of my daughters and my friends. Now that I'm far away, in a monotonous and peaceful environment, I replay everything in my head. I listen each day to all the news broadcasts, and I almost forget I'm no longer there—everything that happens touches me so deeply.

I used to have a routine: my corner chair, for my morning coffee and first cigarette. My apartment, which welcomed me after long days at work. My neighbors, whom I'd chat with about the futile and the essential. I miss everything immensely. Nothing will return as it was.

The key that I brought with me will no longer open any door. A few days after my departure from Gaza, my apartment was gone, with only its skeletal frame remaining. Hit by Israeli artillery, then flattened from inside with grenades. They burned everything. I was sent photos; I have them on my phone. Nothing that I loved there survived. Nothing is salvageable. If I even wanted to rebuild, it would cost an enormous amount. That's what the Israelis do: they destroy but don't raze to the ground. They leave to us even the burden of paying to cart off the rubble.

My sister Samya, who has been living for months in that house, keeping it alive, is still in Gaza City. In the photos she sends me, I almost don't recognize her. She and her family have suffered enormously from lack of food, and even now they aren't eating enough to recover.

My mother, my brother Ahmed with his wife and kids, and my sister Siham with her children are still in the "chalet" in Deir al-Balah. That area too has changed since I've left. They tell me that now, surrounding the building, are thousands of tents. They were set up after the army advanced, when most of the refugees in the South were forced to return to the central zone, eventually taking up every square inch of space. I can't stop thinking about my elderly mother. My siblings told me that when I left, she fell ill. I feel sick too, not knowing if I'll ever see her again, ever hug her again and kiss her on the forehead, like I always do.

My brother Hassan has left Rafah too. With his wife and kids, he's now living in a tent on the western shoreline, together with many of his colleagues from the Red Crescent. Unfortunately, their commitment to humanitarianism isn't enough to protect them. The army continues its operations in that area, and when the bombs fall, they're forced to take refuge in the sea. I'm really worried for them.

Especially for the youngest of his children, Majd, who is barely three and spoiled by everyone. They don't have a good internet connection, so now I only see him in the photos that Hassan keeps sending me. He has a smile that will warm your heart.

The families with whom I shared my fate in Khan Yunis and Rafah are still in that tent city, on the beach that was also supposed to be my shelter. They send me photos every day. Some show architectural solutions to problems solved without me, or new versions of the dishes I used to cook for them. Just to say, we miss you.

There's also another of our friends with them, Mohamad. He's angry and depressed because he paid for a transfer out of Gaza with his loved ones just days before Israeli tanks again closed the Rafah crossing. He lost a great deal in this war. His café in Gaza City had the best coffee in town. There were just a couple of tables, but that's where we would get together, with so many friends. And it was destroyed. He also lost his beautiful apartment, after he'd just moved in. We talk on the phone and try not to cry as we remember distant times that seem so close.

My colleague Sami is still there too. He's suffering, deeply but in silence. He keeps pretending to be too busy with his work as a journalist; it's a way to avoid collapsing and giving way to so much accumulated sadness and anger. But he confides in me how he really feels.

Here in Cairo, among the thousands of Palestinian refugees who got out of the Strip in time, Fatma and her sister Soad are here. Also my friend Mohamad Abu Shaban with his family. And Wesam, a former cameraman. He was among the last to get out—just a few hours before the border was closed on May 6. We see each other frequently to talk. We try to help each other to get past the trauma that we're all suffering from. It's a slow process, but at least I'm no longer weeping alone, in silence.

I don't know what sort of future I'll have. Assuming the war ends and it's possible to return, do I still have enough energy and time for that? I'm fifty-seven years old, and I spent my entire life in an occupied country. Like my father and grandfather before me,

I've never known stability in my homeland. I've also lived under Israeli occupation and under the constant threat of being killed or arrested, deprived of the liberty to go where I want. I've always had the dream of celebrating, one day, the freedom of my people. Yet after October 7, this dream became impossible. Shattered, I fear, also for generations to come. Yet eventually I must leave to them the task of rebuilding.

My Gaza is now only memories. A castle made of words with which I rebuild every street, every face, every emotion. I know it's not the right time to be making decisions, not yet. I try to heal my wounded spirit, putting the pieces of who I once was back together. I try not to spend all my time thinking about what I have lost. Trying not to be a bundle of rage, depression, and hatred.

When I first got to Cairo, on my table, I always kept the keys to my house in Jabalia, the keys to my car, and the keys to my small piece of land in the North. As a reminder that I've lost everything, and that I too share the fate of the Palestinian people.

Today, those keys that no longer open anything have been put away. I put them in a box, in the back of a closet. For now I want to put my life aside. Looking for the place to begin again.

## *ABOUT THE AUTHORS*

SAMI AL-AJRAMI is a Palestinian journalist. Born in Jabalia, the largest refugee camp in the north of the Gaza Strip, he has worked for years as a freelancer for a diverse array of international news organizations. He writes for the Italian news agency ANSA as well as the Italian daily *la Repubblica*. He now lives in Egypt.

ANNA LOMBARDI is an Italian journalist from Rome. She began her career as a freelancer with a variety of news organizations in print and on radio. From 2004, she has worked for the Italian daily *la Repubblica*, first by writing for their weekly news magazine, "Venerdì." As a foreign affairs correspondent, she has reported from Paris, London, and New York.

## *ABOUT THE TRANSLATORS*

JIM HICKS is former executive editor of the *Massachusetts Review* and a former lecturer at the University of Massachusetts Amherst. His most recent translation is Federica Marzi's *My Home Somewhere Else*.

ANNA BOTTA is professor emerita of Italian and Comparative Literature at Smith College.